SAPPHIRE

AMERICAN *Dreams*

SERPENT'S TAIL

HIGH RISK

B O O K S

NEW YORK / LONDON

Lyrics from Bob Dylan's "Sad-Eyed Lady of the Lowlands" © 1966 by Dwarf Music. All rights reserved. International copyright secured. Reprinted by permission.

Grateful acknowledgment is made to the editors of the following publications: *Seems, City Lights Review, Eyeball, Central Park, Conditions, Caprice, Amaranth Review, Brooklyn Review, Outweek, On Our Backs, Common Lives/Lesbian Lives, Sinister Wisdom, Poder, And Then, Queer City: The Portable Lower East Side, COLORLife, Day of Hope, Knitting Factory Knotes, Celebrating Diversity: A Tenth Anniversary Journal by Men of All Colors Together*; and to the editors of the following volumes: *Women on Women: An Anthology of Lesbian Short Fiction* (Plume, 1990); *Loving in FEAR: An Anthology of Lesbian and Gay Survivors of Childhood Sexual Abuse* (Queer Press, 1991); *Our Lives: Lesbian Personal Writings* (Second Story Press, 1991); *Loss of the Ground-note: Women Writing about the Loss of Their Mothers* (Clothespin Fever Press, 1992); *Life Notes: Personal Writings by Contemporary Black Women* (W. W. Norton, 1994); and *High Risk 2* (Plume 1994).

This collection first published 1994 by
High Risk Books/Serpent's Tail
4 Blackstock Mews, London, England N4 2BT
and 401 West Broadway, New York, NY 10012

Book and cover design by Rex Ray
Typeset in 11/15 Janson and Futura Condensed Bold
    by Alabama Book Composition of Deatsville, Alabama
Printed in Hong Kong by Colorcraft, Ltd.

Acknowledgments

Thanks to Harold Augenbraum and the Mercantile Library for a residency at the Writer's Studio, where parts of this book were written.

Many thanks to Terri L. Jewell, Egyirba High, Carletta Walker, Blakmajik Rainbow and Asha Bandele for their help and encouragement with the manuscript along the way.

Thanks to Chava Tuckman and Pam Booker for being good friends.

Special thanks also to my agent, Malaga Baldi, for her belief in me and for being good at what she does.

And very special thanks to my editor, Amy Scholder, whose belief and determination were major factors in bringing this book into being.

Each of our experiences is unique, but there is a commonality. We have to emphasize the common denominators. We cannot afford to become captives of our own pain. Victimization has to be shared—and transcended—together.

—Hanan Ashrawi

You asked me if I ever stood up for anything. Yeah, I stood up for my life.

—Tina Turner

for the child within us all

Contents

Are You Ready to Rock?

. . . nobody said that what was cannot be changed. This is an adventure in light waves & new days tiptoeing across a poisoned land selling flowers to soul survivors. We smile for Tina Turner & those fabulous legs that finally carried her to freedom. We hear you, honey, walking to freedom with thirty-six cents & a gas credit card. *What's Love Got to Do With It* when it leaves you brain damaged, bleeding in the snow, blind, limbless, discarded & deserted. Jerry Hall says you can never be sure your man is not gonna run off & leave you. That's terrible. I'm not being sarcastic. I feel like someone poured acid on my face & is banging in my dreams with telephone poles.

oh oh OH
please don't leave me
please don't leave me
please please please
don't go
baby
please don't go.
thank god for that
black boy from Augusta, GA
who grew up to be a man
running down his yellow wife
beating her bloody with a lead pipe.
yet still, when I hurt
I put that record on—
when I'm in the black hurt
it goes all thru my soul
& I scream:
baby please don't go.
All over women douse themselves with perfume, put
on push-up bras & slide into tight red dresses flashing
the hold card of youth & desirability. With no pity on
paraplegics, heartbroken sharecroppers or stock mar-
ket executives, they creep out back doors into different
colored arms sending knives thru the hearts of men
who owned them. & when you're young & pretty &
you can feel he wants you, you tear his eyes out with
blue syphilis from the back door man cause you know
you a woman who got to bleed every month & finally
turn to sour milk & fat & die alone or too young or
someone will put a gun to your head in a moment of
justifiable passion that the judge understands (after all

how would *he* feel if *his* wife fucked the gardener) &
your brains mingle with the oil stains on the driveway
& your memory is a mantra lesbians & nuns with
shaved heads chant at battered women's shelters.

om nama kali ma
om nama kali ma
wear your love like heaven
but don't leave the woods
Little Red Riding Hood
& if I was you I'd be careful
of grandma too.
oh blue moon
black guitar fingers
string around
your clitoris
scream like broken glass
coca cola bottles
wipe out your vagina
detonating your eyes
into hills Red Cloud
rode across like fire,
after the infantry
burning the cornfields
of a mother's love
who slept while
your father smeared
his dick with ice cream
& entreated you
to suck it.
The world sleeps

under orange dioxin rains
eating tuna fish sandwiches
made of dead dolphins.
no one sees the bruises
not even after I swallow
everything in sight—pills, poison.
no one asks me what's wrong
they tell me I'm crazy
crazy
crazy
Crazy Horse
riding free against the cavalry
Harriet Harriet
Tubman
mumbling
falling out
in the swamp
comin'
comin'
comin' fo'
to carry me
home,
not my mother
not my sister
not my brother
it's me
he did it
to *me*
oh lord

standin' in the
need of prayer,

where were you
oh lord
when I was bleeding
from the asshole
at three years old.
sometimes I feel
like a motherless child
a long
long
long
way
from home.
if dogs run free then why can't we
which way mister
which way to 42nd Street

not my mother
not my father
it's me
it's me
it's me oh lord
standin' on the cement rock
where Mary stood.

oh Mary
don't you weep,
try some crack
against the memory
of your mother
sleeping
while your father was

creeping.
oh Martha
don't you moan,
let me get a snapshot
of you going down
on the dog
& let me tell you
if you don't be a good little girl
I'll show it to everybody.

oh baby please
oh baby please

wear your love like heaven
wear your love like heaven

maybe white men won't be so mean
she thinks as she smears lipstick
on her thick black lips

sliding the comb thru her blonde hair
patting powder on her white cheeks
she thinks, black guys are different
not like my father
at least I can feel 'em
when we fuck,
I couldn't *feel* daddy
even though he ate
up my life

& spit it in my face.

20 years
30 years
38 years
38 years
then you remember
you remember in a dream
or in a classroom full of kids
teaching the difference between
a noun & a pronoun,
you remember over a hamburger
at McDonald's or
someone touches your breast
in a way that seems ancient,
you remember sitting on
the toilet watching your
blood drip red on top of toilet paper & shit,
you remember
reading a poem,
you remember
masturbating.

& your life
is never the same.
Finally
you know.
You know
why you felt
so different

so long,
why you felt
so low
like you shoulda
been flushed
down the toilet
before you were born,
now you know
why you went willingly,
to the back door,
whore house
& white bitch's kitchen
now you know
why you didn't feel
like shit,
couldn't say no,
couldn't ask for what you needed,
couldn't get close
couldn't love anybody
couldn't get your shit together
couldn't market yourself
couldn't believe you could do it
couldn't read
couldn't drive
couldn't stop having babies
or eating
or smoking
or fucking,
now you know
why you are you.

now you know why while dogs ran free
you stayed home,
alone,
looking out the window
of a war zone,
always smiling
or crying
over this man
or that woman.
now you know why
the sky is crying
& maybelline
just couldn't
be true
& Corina
Corina
never
stops
eating
& Little Eva
is a crack head.
now you know why
with a job on Wall Street,
nice white boy husband
& a house in the country
she tore her
wrists apart
& bled into
the nite
dying

alone
on the
bathroom floor
you had scrubbed
earlier that day.
now you know
now you know
& now that you know,
you can begin
to heal.

American Dreams

Suspended in a sea of blue-gray slate
I can't move from the waist down
which brings visions & obsessions of & with
quadriplegics & paraplegics,
wondering how they live, smell,
why they don't just die.
Some people wonder that about blacks,
why they don't just die.
A light-skinned black woman I know
once uttered in amazement about a black black woman
"I wanted to know how did she *live*
being as black as she was!"   11
I don't quite know how to get free
of the karma I've created
but I can see clearly now
that I have created my life.
My right ankle has mud in it,
I'm in debt.
I need dental work
& I am alone.
Alone if I keep seeing myself
through "Donna Reed" & "Father Knows Best" eyes,
if I don't see the friends,
people who care,
giving as much from their lives as they can.
If you live in the red paper valentine of first grade
    in 1956

then you are alone.
If you live in the world of now
of people struggling free
then you are not.

Isolation rises up
like the marble slabs
placed on the front
of cheap concrete high-rises
with apartments that start at 500,000 dollars.
It all seems so stupid
but I understand it now,
why they have homeless people
sleeping in front of these
artificial-penis-looking buildings.
It's so we'll move in,
so such terror will be implanted
in our guts
we'll save our money
& buy a concrete box
to live in & be proud
to call it home.
All anybody really wants
is some security,
a chance to live comfortably
until the next
unavoidable tragedy
unavoidably hits them
& splices open their chests,
& takes the veins from their legs,
& carves up their heart

in the name of surgery
or vicious murder
murder
murderer
ha! ha! ha!
murderer.
No one,
nothing
can protect you
from the murderer.
Not the police, nuclear weapons, your mother, the
Republicans, mx missiles—
none of that
can protect you
from the murderer.
Even if you get all the niggers
out the neighborhood
the murderer might be
a white boy like David Berkowitz
baby-faced Jewish boy
who rarely missed a day
of work at the post office.
ha! ha! ha!
you're never safe!
Like a crab walking sideways
America hides its belly
under an arsenal of radioactive crust,
creeping along with its
long crustacean eyes,
stupid & blind
sucking debris from

the ocean floor
till there is no more,
while the giant Cancer breasts
get biopsied & amputated
& the crab caves in
under the third world's dreams
& 5 million pounds of concrete.
& the murderer
stabs stabs stabs
at the underbelly &
submicroscopic
viruses
fly out
in
ejaculate
& claim
your life,
while the powers that don't be
join
for a loving circle jerk
& nostalgic reminiscence
of days gone by,
lighting candles for Roy Cohn
& J. Edgar Hoover
as they lay a bouquet of cigarettes
on John Wayne's grave
who is clandestinely slipping
into the wax museum
to suck Michael Jackson's dick
only to find he has had his penis
surgically reconstructed

to look like Diana Ross's face.
& the Trane flies on
like Judy Grahn's wild geese
over a land diseased like cancer
killing flowers by the hour
& a huge hospice
opens up in the sky
& the man quietly tells his wife
as he picks up his rifle,
"I'm going people hunting."
& he steps calmly
into McDonald's & picks off
20 people
& blood pours red
Big Macs fall flat
to the floor amid
shrieks & screams
while a plastic clown
smiles down on the house
additives & the destruction of
the rain forests built.
& you smile for a while
feeling ever so American
& in good company
as you eat compulsively.
After all,
the whole country does it.
It's just pasta heaven here
till you get your x-ray
or biopsy back.
Making the world safe

for democracy
& you can't even evade
heart disease
until you're 40,
& it attacks quietly
walking on those big
expensive sneakers
niggers wear
as they shove the pawn shop gun
to your head & say,
"GIMME EVERYTHING YOU GOT!"
& for once you are not afraid
cause the nigger has AIDS.
You laugh triumphantly,
finally you've given him
& the world
everything you got!

I was at Clark Center for the Performing Arts
getting ready for my morning ballet class
when this old wrinkled-up white faggot
ran up to me, threw his arms around me & grabbed me
in a vise-like grip & screamed:
BE MY BLACK MAMMY SAPPHIRE
BE MY BLACK MAMMY
He held on & wouldn't let go.
Finally I thought to turn
my hand into a claw
& raked straight down his face
with my fingernails.
He let go.

I'll never forget how
hurt & bewildered he looked.
I guess he was just playing.
I was just devastated.

There are no words
for some forms
of devastation
though we constantly
try to describe
what America has done
& continues to do to us.
We try to describe it
without whining
or quitting
or eating french fries
or snorting coke.
It's so hard not
to be an addict in America
when you know numerology
& have x-rayed the inside
of Egyptian mummies 5,000 years old
& robbed the graves of Indians
deliberately blinded children
& infected monkeys & rats
with diseases you keep alive
waiting for the right time
so you can spring 'em
on anyone who might be making progress.

Well, you're miserable now America.
The fact you put a flag

on the moon
doesn't mean you own it.
You can't steal everything
all the time
from everybody.
You can't have the moon, sucker.

A peanut farmer
warned
you could not stay number 1;
number 1 being an illusion
in a circle, which is
what the world is,
but you still think that
the world is flat
& you can drive out evil
with a pitchfork & pickup truck.

One time when I was a little girl living on an army base
I was in the gymnasium & the general walked in.
& the general is like god or the president, if you believe.
The young woman who was supervising
the group of children I was with said,
"Stand up everybody! The general's here!"
Everybody stood up except me.
The woman looked at me & hissed,
"Stand up for the general!"
I said, "My father's in the army, not me."
& I remained seated.
& throughout 38 years

of bucking & winging
grinning & crawling
brown nosing & begging
there has been a quiet
10 year old in me
who has remained seated.
She perhaps is the real American Dream.

Mickey Mouse Was a Scorpio

the night was no light,
black.
he came in
light cracking the night
stuck in the doorway
of dark
deep hard.
my father,
lean in blue & white striped pajamas,
snatches my pajama bottoms off
grabs me by my little skinny knees
& drives his dick in.
i scream
i scream
no one hears except my sister
who becomes no one cause she didn't hear.
years later i become no one cause it didn't happen
but it's night now & it's happening,
a train with razor blades for wheels
is riding thru my asshole
iron hands saw at my knees
i'm gonna die
i'm gonna die
blood, semen & shit gush from my cracked ass.
my mother, glad not to be the one,
comes in when it's over to wash me.
she is glad glad,

satanic glad.
she brings her hand up from between my legs &
smears shit, semen & blood over my mouth,
"Now she'll know what it's like to have a baby,"
    she howls.
drugged night so black
you could paint with it,
no moon   no stars   no god.
the night stick smashes my spinal cord,
my legs
bleeding bandages of light
fall off.
let me go
let me go
don't tell me about god & good little girls
i want to live
i want to live
my cells crack open like glass
the bells are tolling for me
my name disintegrates in the night
God's a lie
this can't be true.
M-I-C-K-E-Y M-O-U-S-E
mother is house (we have a nice house
California ranch style)
brother is the nail
we drive thru your heart
do it
do it to her, brother.
M-I-C-K-E-Y M-O-U-S-EEE
mouse is in the house

running thru my vagina
& out my nose.
saucer-eyed bucktooth child
Betsy Wetsy
brown bones
electrocuted.
Tiny Tears
that never dry
hopscotch
hickory dock
the mouse fell off
the clock
the farmer takes Jill down the well
& all the king's horses
& all the king's men
can't put that baby together again.
crooked man
crooked man
pumpkin eater
childhood stealer.

in my father's house

1.

together alone one night we were watching t.v.
& my father shot to his feet as
   The Star Spangled Banner
hailed the network's last gleaming.
he stood at attention saluting the red & white striped
tongue gyrating on the t.v. screen.
"Daddy," I said, "you don't have to do that."
"I know I don't have to but I want to," he said.

my mother slipped on her sweater & disappeared.
we rolled loose to corners of the room.
buttoned in cold; bones of children knitting
   shadows in the dark,
dreaming of pullovers, cardigans, cashmere & mohair.
"She never wanted children," he explained.

he told me his father put his foot on his neck
& beat him until his nose bled.
he left home when he was 14,
an Aries full of blind light
trying to wrap barbed wire around the wind.

my father bent a piece of rubber hose
into a black ellipse, then taped the ends together
to make a handle. he beat me with this.

I was grown, in my own apartment,
when the cat sprang up on my record player
claws gouging Bob Marley's *Burnin' & Lootin'*.
I snatched that cat off the record player
slammed it to the floor,
beat skin, teeth, skull with my fists,
tied its legs together & yanked its tail back
exposing the anus, tiny fist curled pink,
I picked up a burning cigarette from the ashtray
& started to stick it up that cat's asshole—
something stopped me.

spliced between the blind night of a forgotten scream
it would be 10 years before I remembered
my father breaking open my asshole.
the memory would walk up behind me like bad news,
as unbelievable as Mayor Goode dropping a bomb
    on Osage Avenue,
as unbelievable as doctors betting on how much
    oxygen it would take
to blind a baby in an incubator then turning up
    the oxygen to see.
it would come like the nurse in the Tuskegee syphilis
    night,
basket full on magic light, lies & placebos.
it would come counter-clockwise like bent swastikas.
it came just when I was learning to stand, to speak.
it grabbed me by my knees & dragged me down the
    years
stopping where I disappeared 35 years ago.

2.

we had a tree,
an avocado tree.
first my father painted it
then he killed it.
even before he decided
to cut the postage stamp–size
swimming pool
into the lawn,
he downed the tree.
I was gone then,
gone long & gone far.
but denial & amnesia
made me send father's day & birthday cards.
in one card I asked,
as I rarely did,
for something:
some avocados.
I said send me
some avocados
from the tree, Daddy.
I got $20 in the mail
& instructions to go
buy some avocados.
he didn't tell me
what he had done
to the tree.

3.

I say you raped me
you say it's a damn lie

you remember being a boy
running after rabbits in Texas
fast as the grass
tall as the sun

crazy slut of a life leaves you with 4 kids & no wife,
3 gone bad
1 just like you:
an achiever
a star
a homeowner
a heterosexual
an athlete
who buys a Mercedes
for his wife & a Porsche
for himself.
a son shining
finally like you.

you fill the rooms
with him,
blue ribbons
& trophies fall
off the wall,

but strange whispers crawl
off the pages of the
local colored tabloid
to the *New York Times*:
they say
this youngest boy rapes,
humiliates women.
he is tried,
but acquitted—
you know how
women lie.

4.

at 14 I cooked, cleaned
no one asked how school was going,
what I needed or dreamed.
I had to have dinner ready at 5:30
biscuits cornbread ribs chicken meatloaf
I was cooking dinner one night
& my father offered to help me
as he sometimes did,
relieving me of some small task.
that night he offered to set the table.
the food was hot, ready to eat,
my little brother had just come in
from football practice,
I went to sit down at the table
& stopped shocked.
my father had only set a place

for himself & my little brother.
"I thought you had already eaten," he offered.
I made no move to get another plate,
neither did he.
he served his son
the food I had prepared.
they ate,
I disappeared,
like the truth
like the tree.

5.

I crawl from under
childhood's
dark table,
black tree
bleeding
spiraling to apogee,
broke doll yawning:
ma ma   ma ma
childhood consumed.
black moon
rising,
eating up
the sky,
a survivor—
heading home,
to my own house.

boys love baseball (or a quarter
boys a lot in 1952)

the little boy
gets into the car
with father.
father drives,
father drives the car
fast.
father drives the car fast fast.
it scares the little boy
it excites the little boy,
little boys like to be scared
little boys like to be excited.
the car is brown.
it is a Pontiac.
can you spell that?
P-O-N-T-I-A-C.
that's right,
Pontiac.
father is driving the brown Pontiac.
that's right,
father is driving.

the little boy is riding
the little boy is riding in the car
the little boy is riding in the car to the baseball game
with father.
his sister is at home
with mother

getting her hair burned
& playing with dolls.
girls love dolls,
boys don't.
boys love baseball,
girls don't.

the car stops
the car stops in the light
the car stops in the light on the road.
only father can stop the car
only father can start the car.
father lifts the boy from the passenger seat
& pulls his pants down.
something hard hurts the boy
for the rest of his life,
splits the soft brown skin
of his buttocks and pushes him in.
father is fucking
father is fucking the boy in the light
father is fucking the boy in the light
stopped on a road.

father gives the boy a quarter.
a quarter buys a lot in 1952.

the little boy's mother had dressed him
so carefully (navy-blue short pants, milk white shirt,
bow tie, new shoes)
so he would look nice on Sunday
when he went to the baseball game

with father.
when she asks,
"What happened to him?"
father is going to say the little boy
peed on himself, that the little boy didn't
speak up and say he had to go
to the bathroom.
it's not father's fault the little boy
doesn't look like a picture anymore.

father did the best he could!
why, no one ever took *father* to the baseball game
when he was a little boy.
why, when father was a little boy
they didn't even let black people
play on the same team as white people.

father is thoroughly disgusted with the little boy.
father is not taking the little boy anywhere
ever again.
why, next Sunday, after Mass,
after the Latin speaks in the priest for 30 minutes,
the little girl,
in her freshly ironed curls,
will go riding, riding with father.

Reflections from Glass Breaking

I CAN BARELY see over the dashboard. Daddy and I are riding in the car through a pretty land like cartoons with giant rabbits, pink flowers and green hills all around. Riding with Daddy is fun. I laugh to be riding with Daddy. But I'm scared, too. Sometimes Daddy changes to a nervous mean man with a tight face. He gives me a white tablet and red sticky stuff in a paper cup to drink. Tastes good. We go to a house, it is empty. Daddy takes me up the stairs. The sunlight is shiny and bright on the pretty wood floor. Green curtains float like flowered dreams at the window. When I look over at Daddy he's leaning in the doorway, his pants are unzipped, his thing is out, and he has stuff like whipped cream on it. He calls me to him, then he grabs my head and pushes his thing in my mouth. I choke and pull away.

Daddy leaves. When he comes back he has zipped-up pants but his face looks nervous and mean. He drags me into the middle of the room, presses me down on the floor and pulls my underpants off. He unzips his pants and takes out his thing. He pushes his floppy thing between my legs. What is he trying to do? His smell climbs up my nose, his black whiskers needle me. His thing is hard now. He pushes his thing, forces his thing in me, and my pelvis cracks. I can't breathe. I hear Daddy saying, "Your Mama said it's alright. Hush. Be a good girl." My eyes close, my head rolls to the side and drops into black. I float up to the ceiling and from far away I see a child's bones come loose and float away in a river of blood as a big man thrusts his thing into a little girl again and again. Then the man pulls his thing out of the little girl, gets up off the floor fast and runs away.

I float down from the ceiling back into my body and open my eyes. The green curtains look like flags at half mast and the sun seems old. Where's Daddy? What happened? A cool breeze from the open window rushes over me and I feel a wetness around my hips. Scared I have peed on myself I put my left hand in the puddle spreading from under the broken bowl of my hips. It is cold. I raise my hand to my face, it is glistening with blood. I put my hand down and stare at the light disappearing on the hardwood floor.

33

Rabbit Man

1.

he's the night
chasing rabbits,
a pot of dust
under the asphalt sky
cracked with stars.
athlete,
'colored boy from Houston makes good.'
standing straight as a razor
he cuts my vagina open
stretches it like bleeding lights thru dark air
his rabbit teeth drag my tongue
over sabers hidden in salt,
from the slit tip
red roses drip
screaming: daddy *don't*.

I'm not supposed to be
your dinner nigger.
your semen forms fingers
in my throat,
furry fingers.
I cough all the time
rabbit man
colored boy
run

jump
hurdle after hurdle—
higher.

till your penis melts
like a marshmallow in fire
and your fear is a desert with no flowers
except two daughters,
American Beauties,
tight rosebuds you hew open,
petals of pink light left bleeding
under a broken moon.
pine needles spring up in the sand
but you don't ask what they're for
surrounded like you are by infant daughters,
little dog fish drowning in diapers.
you did this rabbit dick,
rabbit dick
rabbit dick
hopping coprophagous freak
blind eyes opening
like terminal disease
in mouth after mouth—
paralyzing light.

2.

I slide between cold polyester rooms,
into your bed—
everything is so cheap and falling apart.

I recoil from the blond skin and
bleeding blue eyes of Jesus.
most nights you slept
in the obituary of light—
alone.
the picture is positioned
so when your head hit the pillow
you saw Jesus.
then what?

3.

you saw death like the black legs of your mother
like the bent teeth of your retarded sister
like the wet smell of light in a fish's eye.
you saw death riding without a car or credit cards.
you saw death creeping waddling like the fat women
    you hated.
you saw Jesus could not save you.

god's hand is creased with the smell of burnt hair and
    hot grease,
she hears you tell your sons don't get no
    black nappy-head woman.
her titties sag down sad snakes that crawl up your legs
till your penis talks and with blind sight you see
the two daughters you left in the desert without water.
oh death knows you and invites you for dinner,
rolls out the driveway like a coupe de ville,
is a snake-tongued daughter who turns on you,

is a thirsty rabbit choking on a lonely road.
death is an ax in an elevator rising to the sun.
death is god's egg.
death is a daughter who eats.
you are the table now the wet black earth lays upon—
you are dinner for dirt,
a cadillac spinning back to a one-room shack.
you are the rabbit released from fear,
the circle broken by sun
the handle of a buried ax,
head rolling thru the desert
like tumbleweed—
back to Neptune.

4.

now I am the queen of sand,
wind wrapping like wire around the rabbit's neck,
the end of a cycle.
my children refuse to believe your penis is a lollipop.
my children are the desert in bloom
cactus flowers opening to forgiveness,
millions of rabbits hopping—
hopping over you.

Trilogy

one

The sky is cryin' look at the tears roll down the trees
—Elmore James

JUST GOT OFF work, country dude—I shouldn't say that, he's nice, real nice—took me to the station. I was thinking weird thoughts all night while I was dancing—this train is so cold, I got wool tights, overalls, leotard, pullover, army jacket—weird thoughts about suicide and shooting myself, going to get me something to eat, something low, greasy worm-ham or pork chops, biscuits, butter pancakes, eggs, going to the hotel with the broad at the bar. She was brown, smooth-skinned, in a dress, hair pressed, makeup, fat. I think she was looking for a man, maybe money, maybe both. I was thinking of going to the hotel and not making love, my mind wasn't on that—but killing ourselves, a joint suicide. I'm not really depressed. I just don't see no progress. I feel old, degenerate, fat, saggy. I wouldn't put it in my mouth, the gun, but to the side of my head. Either way it'd probably be a closed-casket funeral. I don't really like myself.

I have been on a long journey twenty-seven years walking backwards. The rent is due next week. I just paid the motherfucker! It's always something—rent, phone, gas, Graham technique classes, tokens. I laid down and spread my legs for them funky, chump-change tips. Into the pink. I saw this fat dude I tricked with at this private party. That bastard could fuck. He took too long to come though. I don't think he ever did, come that is, least not with me.

Is this a poem? I mean, is there any beauty in this twenty-seven-year-old black bitch riding the tube home from New Jersey three o'clock in the morning? Is all the beauty in the stars?

DUE TO LOCAL TRACK MAINTENANCE SOUTHBOUND D TRAINS ARE RUNNING ON 8TH AVENUE. THOSE DESIRING SOUTH-BOUND SERVICE SHOULD CATCH THE NORTHBOUND TRAIN TO 59TH STREET. WE ARE SORRY FOR THE INCONVENIENCE. The elevator is broke. I'm sitting here writhing in hate thinking about Smitty who took my poems, $100, and my picture six months ago talking about he was gonna publish my book. I hate these men where I dance. One black nigger, disgusting cussing slick son of a bitch, hands all over me, free feels. I was scared to kick him in the teeth like I wanted to. I could see his insane reaction. I could see my wig flying off, teeth knocked out, lip bruised, bloodied, because of a lifetime of failure, his crumpled losses, reduced specimen of a human being. He had this crumpled piece of paper he was pretending was a dollar so he could stick it in my g-string so he could touch me. I hate the sight of these filthy chimpanzee dick bastards. Rage chokes me, wears me. I am humiliated daily. I feel apprehensive about reading this aloud. Would you? If it were your poem, your life—if it was cold, going on four in the morning and your neck was contorted in hate and pain. If someone speaks to me I will start screaming. I sound like other poems I've read, other women I've felt, listened to.

I can't hardly *breathe* for the wine in the air. If you could see these early morning linty-head, green pants wearing dejections; these pieces of shit got the nerve to try to hit on someone. I won't cry next time I read about one of these motherfuckers freeze to death. Rock gut syphilitic sons of bitches got the nerve to leer at somebody. Cobweb red eyes. I'm exhausted. There is no express service at night. I want the world to die.

two

Don't pull no subway. I rather see you pull a train . . .
                                        —Jimmy Reed

I had done a party
for Carl,
another one of those
bachelor parties,
nothing really unique—
regular crowd,
working class,
basement, red lights,
gin. I had got

drunk off that
gin so I could loosen up
and do my
thing;
freaked off the
Rolling Stones'
Miss You,
got down with the Spinners'
He'll Never Love You Like I Do
and
Love Don't Love Nobody.
Yeah, me and this
other bitch
was doin' it
to the 't'
gettin' 'em hard

and horny.
No tips,
75 off the top
plus whatever we could
get in tricks.
Sometimes I do good
on the trick side
sometimes I don't.
When it's a white set
I usually get over
or if it's niggers
and I ain't got
no hard competition
(latin or white)
I might do alright.
But this night
was kinda
the pits,
I had got 20
outta Carl;
and Teresa,
the other bitch,
was cleaning up.
So now Teresa was
getting down with
the groom-to-be,
the one they was
giving the party for,
and he says, 'Hows about
both of you,
how much would it cost

to get down with
both of you?'
and I said, 'Just
gimme 20 honey
and we can get it on,'
like that, you know,
I was cool.
Anyway I felt like
the hoe was being greedy
and I knew he had already
upped 20 for her,
so it wasn't like
I was cuttin' in
on nothin'.
We both humped him

for a tic,
he was taking a while to come,
a little head woulda
done it,
but Teresa wasn't
into that
and I didn't want to
rank her shit,
plus she had more business
to take care of
so we just pushed
him off.
He was kinda pissed
so I started rappin'
telling him how he was
such a heavy dude

the two of us
couldn't make him come,
how most of our tricks
usually come in 3 minutes
and how unique he was and shit.
Then we went in the bathroom
and started talking,
bout his getting married,
jogging, he jogged,
he was only 27
and how he'd always wanted to,
or thought he would
marry someone tall light skinny,
or not too heavy,
with plenty ass and tits.
And how she was
dark chubby
and didn't give head;
he'd met her
and said in a month
he'd fuck her
forget her,
but something happened.
And about his job
$14 an hour in a factory,
he did some chemical shit
high risk,
the bosses don't give a fuck
long as they hauling
in the buck,
I mean one little slip

and they could all be
blown to bits,
but you know
you need that job thang;
everything has risks
he told me,
just like the trip
you're doing,
someone could just
go OFF on you.
And he asked me
did I have to deal
with men who was
old and ugly and fat.
and I asked
what he'd do if just say
you know, he hadn't hooked up
and had plenty bucks.
and he said like if I
won the lottery or some shit?
I said yeah.
And he said, 'Oh
I would probably do
like photography,
not women and stuff
but animals and nature.
Just then, someone started
banging on the bathroom door
talkin' bout, 'Hey man
where's the girl? Hell,
you gonna keep her
all night!'

three

Go head pretty baby, honey knock yourself out . . .
—Jimmy Reed

P is for Princess, the Original Bronze Beauty of Show
World. It's for pretty titties, generosity, and a weird
honesty. I remember the first time I saw her, she had
on a long Indian-looking wig, cheap sharp vines,
makeup, heels swishing, hostile, arrogant. Sixteen.
Holding her windows. A peep show queen. Unh huh,
a freak for white boys, blonds. Hated niggers. Shocked
me with her sickness. Told me she hated black men,
niggers. I was still new, able to be shocked, not in total
understanding, not knowing the circle unbroken I
would end up well worked and insane too. And we
became close. She was real. I liked her body. It was me,
Sherry, Naomi, Lee, Princess, Misty, Angel, Zulima,
Shawneesy, RubyJune—stripping, jammed into that
little dressing room, a world to itself, a freak set
untouched by outside values. I learned to be free, to
like their bodies, play. The men in the booths, the
freaks, I watched them drop quarters, crook their
fingers, beckon, unzip their pants. Sticking out their
tongues, pointing to their dicks, OOHH they would
go as they begged us to look, as if it was something
good. We laughed at them as they looked at us. They
jacked off, rolling their eyes, shaking, pissing in the

booths. Rasta men, Hasidic Jews, Asian businessmen, slick young-looking niggers, bowing before a need in the booth. We needed the money.

I was new in town. The dude I was staying with, who was a friend of my girlfriend's new boyfriend, worked there as a projectionist, first took me there. I was wigged, made up, told Lee, the manager, yes, I had danced, could dance, would audition. She told me O.K., but she didn't need no dancers not till October, but I needed then. She told me she needed a 'love team' now. I said, cool. I had a partner, I told her. The dude I was staying with told me about a dude he knew was game. We hooked up. Money. I needed money. We "rehearsed" at his ol' lady's house. Came back. Lee said we was a good love team. She liked us. She used me in between my act too. I would go out there and dance with the girls, help 'em do their shows. It was fun but she didn't pay me. Lee ran so much game trying to get sales up. Worked us. She was a big Hottentot butt woman, ex-secretary/singer who'd slipped into the business. She told everyone she was a virgin. I don't know, it sounded weird to me. I never said anything, she was responsible for the paychecks, the bookings. I held onto my dreams, talked, found myself to be like everybody else. Whatever else I thought, I was still there showing pussy like everybody else.

It was another world, Naomi, nineteen (she said), Puerto Rican—(swore on nine Bibles she was Polynesian). Told me she was from Polynesia. But I know the South Bronx when I see it. That girl was obsessed with the buck. Said she wanted to get twenty grand in the bank. She worked her ass off from ten in the morning to twelve at night, sometimes three in the morning. Only took off to get costumes, makeup, go to the bank or Mass. The bitch went to Mass on Sunday, Lee too, religious like that, but you know, Naomi swore she wasn't gay. Too hard, she protested, too hard. I knew better. Her and Sherry became lovers. It was a fantasy world, the women. Actually we only made three dollars and fifty cents a show and usually only did one show an hour (that we got paid for, that is. Lee had us out there humping a lot for free, "doubling" she called it, "Why don't you help so and so, she's losing her windows"). But we worked twelve hours a day, seventeen on weekends and lots of time there were too few girls so we'd get in a lot of extra shows. It wasn't nothin' to come out with four, five bills a week, but still.

Misty and I—we liked each other. We all did teams together—lesbian love teams. It was fun. I liked doing it with Sherry, Princess, Misty—not Naomi so much, she twisted, flipped like a fish. She always perfumed her pussy, I didn't like that. We usta freak off on the mike while we was doin' teams. Talk crazy shit like fuckin' Dobermans and a little house in the country, just my woman and me. And ooh fist fuck me, beat me. Crazy stupid shit. Sometimes the customers liked it, sometimes they didn't. One time me and Sherry was on stage and I was saying something like, Do it to me wit a bottle honey. I mean regular routine bull. And

Misty rushed out on stage like a mad thing with a coke bottle. Weird. Maybe she was high. So you want a bottle? She was serious. I had to use all my strength, she woulda jammed me if she could. I felt different toward her after that. Me and Sherry both said later, Whew! She's a little off. She was really serious! Golden showers! The customers wanted to see golden showers! I pissed on Princess once on stage. I felt weird after that. She said, Lemme do it to you. I said no. I know how she felt. Tina, this white broad, one of the manager's girlfriends, asked me to pee on her too. She was for real, heavy into S&M, usta come to work with bruises. That's how she got off. She was around forty, yeah, at least. She had kids, three or four of them. Pornography is a trip. No big thing. We all got freak in us. Men are so weird. The dudes who come in those booths—slaves like. I'm glad my sex thang ain't like that. I'm glad I ain't got to pay.

Christina Dawn Santana was thirty-eight. She'd come out and tell you how old she was. She was a trip. Boy that bitch could suck a dick. I had never seen a woman like that before. She blew my mind. She had a crush on the dude who I was doing the love team with, would ask me to let her do my shows. I'd be glad. I hated it. She loved it. Didn't like to fuck though. She was only into oral sex. She'd suck him off then parade around the stage flexing her biceps. She'd make him come again and again. We watched amazed. I had never seen such a voracious woman. He begged off. He was drained, dry, weak. She exhausted him. I had never seen that before, always I had seen niggers begging for more. Christina would get drunk offa that rum. She liked me. But I couldn't relate. Unh uh, not my thing. Now Zulima, she was fine. Built, brown-skinned, solid, lesbian to her heart. Dressed nice. A data processor during the day, love teams at night. Couldn't stand it either, talked about how it feels to be a lesbian and have a man's hands on you four, five, ten, twelve times a day! I ate her pussy on stage, no fake simulation shit, we got on down! She turned out to be into masculine types though.

The real bosses was Mafia men (least that's what everybody said). We didn't see 'em though. A lot of the employees, projectionists and shit, was foreigners, West Indians and Africans, too. Show World didn't take taxes out the girls' checks and we, most of the girls, used phony names and social security numbers. Misty was married to an East Indian dude darker than me who hated niggers. Both Angel's parents were Black Muslims. She was born a Muslim, married a white Irish dude. Shawneesy married this French Canadian dude named Peter. It used to trip me out—the black girls and white men. Now I under-stand. I understand good. Wigs, costumes, toenails, and g-strings. Music. Isaac Hayes sing some sexy songs. We usta play the hell outta Isaac Hayes. You could drown in the business. It's like dope or jail. Some people get in and never get out. Either way you're never the same.

P is for Princess
popcorn
pornography
powerless
people
pimp
pander
peanut
pretty
plump
promise
prone
position
pussy
piece

Penthouse
Players
Playboy
pink
pimples
pleasure
perverted
peter
pissed
putrid
promise
perfume
pearls
put out
put on
put off

P is for Princess
pornography
prostitution
powerless
people
pawns
pimped

A New Day for Willa Mae

ONE STEP AT A time, she told herself, one hand over her heart, the other on the banister, a large tote bag on each shoulder. "Yes!" she exclaimed softly, "the storm is passin' ovah! Yes Lord, the storm is passin' ovah." She lifted a large leg to the next step. In this fashion, one step at a time, calling on the Lord when needed, she made it to her apartment on the third floor. Her and her daughter's, she reminded herself.

"Whew!" she exhaled loudly as she placed both bags on the floor and reached inside her worn vinyl purse for her keys. Wiping perspiration from her brow she unlocked the door, then bent over to pick up her bags at the same time pushing the door open with her large rear end. "Lord, them steps gonna be the death of me yet," she sighed. Her daughter appeared in the hallway opposite the front door. She stood and looked at her mother's huge white-uniformed body, the beige polyester coat coming apart at the seam under one arm, her big bosom, her huge stomach that fell into the large apron of flesh that rested on top of her thighs, the flesh crammed in white stockings. She looked at her mother's burnished brown gourd of a face, her eyes black holes with smoky circles of fatigue painted under them. She looked at the beads of sweat on her forehead and told her contemptuously, "Mama, you oughtta lose some weight."

Willa Mae Justice looked at her daughter and said with astonishment in her soft voice, "Youse the only somethin' I know goes roun' tellin' they Mama what she oughtta do. You set them limas to boil and make the rice and cornbread like I asked you?"

"I forgot the bread, Mama."

"Well, why don't you do that steadda standin' there lookin' at me."

Willia Mae handed her daughter a bag full of mustard, collard and turnip greens. She took the other shopping bag down the hall to her room which was at the end of the hall past the bathroom and Jadine's room.

Things became a little less burdensome when she stepped into the large quiet room with the big strong mahogany bed Johnson, her first husband, had bought. It was made up in the stark white sheets Mrs. Goldstein had given her when she switched over to the designer ones with flowers and cubes printed on them.

Willa Mae looked at the quilt on the bed, dark blue wool bordered with black velvet; in the center of the quilt was a large circle of the black velvet. She didn't have time or the mind to quilt up here, but she had known what she was doing when she made that one. The circle had spoken to her many times with its black voice telling her to relax, that there was more to the whole thing than she could see, and that trouble, indeed, did not last always. The quilt had been packed in her trunk till Jadine was five or six or so, then she'd remembered it when Johnson left. She had taken the red imitation satin quilt Johnson had given her and tried to give it to Mrs. Goldstein; after all, Mrs. Goldstein had given Willa Mae so many nice things. That was when Mrs. Goldstein began to think Willa Mae might be very different from the previous colored girls. But Willa Mae wasn't that different, she'd been relieved to find out later, just another large colored girl with a child she had to feed, benign contempt for the people she served, clean, a good cook, a little late sometimes, and never available Wednesday evenings or Sundays.

Willa Mae took off her worn white work shoes and sat on the side of the bed. She lifted the bag onto her lap and took out the box. Shoes, *New Balance*, $49.99, pretty shiny blue nylon and soft white suede. But my god! Forty-nine dollars! They may as well jus' gone say fifty dollars! But Jadine's feet was gonna fall off if she ran in them ones she had anymore and the man had said these was the best. She cocked her head listening to the belligerent sounds of Jadine fixing dinner, heaved to her feet and padded barefoot down the hall to Jadine's room. She placed the box by Jadine's bed.

Back on her bed Willa Mae pulled the bag up on her lap and took out a tissue-wrapped package. Carefully she opened it, gazed in delight at the mound of red lace and satin. She shook the slip, looked at it, and fingered the lace. "Now, when have I had something like this!" she exclaimed. She got up and locked her bedroom door. Then she pulled off her uniform and her slip; letting her breasts fall out of her brassiere, she stepped in front of her dressing table and looked at her large body with satisfaction. "It's mine," she sighed. She pulled the new slip over her head. As the smooth material fell over her hips she began to twirl around, air gathering under the frothy, flared bottom of the slip causing it to fan out as she danced. She wasn't so old, she thought, gazing at herself in the mirror. Forty-six wasn't old. She smiled at herself in the mirror, then took the slip off, folded it, and put it in her dresser drawer. She was closing the drawer when Jadine called, "Mama! Dinner's ready!"

Willa Mae sat across from Jadine and asked, "What we got, daughter?"

"Salad, beans, rice and cornbread."

"No meat?"

"No, Mama, no meat. You know I don't eat meat."

"Well you not the only someone eating."

"Mama!"

"Jadine!"

"Every time I try to say something it's JayDEEN!"

"What are you trying to say?"

"We don't *need* meat."

"What do we need?"

"The amino acids."

"The *whats*?"

"The amino acids is what makes up protein and they in almost everything. Beans got 'em, rice got 'em. And the rice got the ones the beans don't have and the beans got the ones the rice don't have. Cornmeal, flour, egg, milk—all that went into the cornbread, that's enough protein for a thousand people!"

"Not no *thousand* Jadine, and Dr. Harris says—"

"Oh, Mama, fuck Dr. Harris! Look at him! How he gonna tell anybody anything?"

"Well, I ain gonna fuck Dr. Harris—"

"Oh, Mama, you know what I mean!"

"No I don't, cause to me fuck mean to fuck and if you don't mean that use another word."

"Oh, Mama, you never listen!"

"I *am* listening to you!"

"You hear what you wanna hear!"

"Jadine, it's time for you to be gettin' a job."

"I got a job. I'm a dancer and marathoner. Aren't you proud of me?"

"Don't none of it put no amino acids on the table. You can't make no money *runnin'*. Same with this dancin'. I'm not talkin' about personal satisfaction, I know you gets that. I'm talkin' about *rent*, utilities, phone bill. At least pay your own phone bill. When I was twenty-six—"

"When you was twenty-six you had *had* me and was

on your own, had come to New York City and found out what *hard* was, you hear me," Jadine mockingly repeated what Willa Mae had told her many times.

"Well, it's the truth!"

"Well, Mama, what do you want me to do? I'm just gettin' into dancing! You want me to have a baby out of wedlock like you—"

"Wedlock! You sound like white folks, Jadine. I been married, jus' wadn't to him. It ain no sin to have a baby by a fool, but to marry him sho is."

"You make me sick, talkin' about Daddy like that! You the fool! He just didn't want you."

"Well, I really don't know. But if you love your Daddy so much you sure can go to him."

"You don't want me!" Jadine screamed, "You never did!"

"You think I'm gonna sit here and let you insult me?"

Jadine pushed her chair back from the table.

"You didn't eat nuthin'."

"I'm not hungry, Mama. How can I digest my food with you talkin' to me like that."

"Well, eat later."

"Mama, sometimes I really don't like you."

"You don't like yourself sometime."

Jadine didn't answer her mother. She was walking out the kitchen now down the hall to her bedroom. Jadine's room was painted lavender with gold trim, milk crates full of books and records lined the walls. A bicycle leaned against the closet door. There was no furniture in her room except a chest of drawers and a box spring and mattress that sat on the floor. It was all she needed. She'd decided a long time ago if you really wanted something, you had to sacrifice. That's what Mama didn't understand. It was a sacrifice for her to still be here. She could get a job and help Mama or get her own place but she couldn't do that if she wanted to keep on dancing. Plus Mama would be lonely if she wasn't here. She didn't see the shoes till she had flung herself on the bed. "Oh Mama!" she gasped softly, "*New Balance*." She sat up on the side of the bed, stretched out her long legs, then slid her feet into the powder blue and white shoes. She padded into the kitchen where her mother sat quietly eating dinner. Seeing her daughter she looked up. "That was some good salad, Jadine. Don't bother with the dishes, I'll get 'em."

"Mama, the shoes!"

"Chile, them ones you had was fallin' apart."

"Thank you, Mama." She looked at her mother in her bathrobe. Her hands were clasped in her lap now and a certain tightness grabbed her neck that would not leave until Jadine left the room.

"Mama, why you drinking coffee this late?"

"Is it late daughter?"

"Seven-thirty."

"It's not that late. Anyhow, I'm expecting Mr. Henry in a while."

"Oh well," she sighed. "Thank you for the shoes, Mama. I really appreciate 'em."

"It's alright Jadine, it's alright."

WILLA MAE SAT back on the clean white sheets, propped up on one elbow, her legs curled under her, the slip against her body, damp with perspiration, the lace finding a home around her knees, molding itself to her breasts. The smooth satin over her stomach made it look like a shiny red beach ball falling from under her breasts. She watched Mr. Henry take off his shirt, undershirt, belt, pants, socks. He walked to her dresser, set his wallet and watch on top, and asked Willa Mae, "Lemme switch out this overhead light here and put on this little one on top de dresser."

Willa Mae was still as Mr. Henry slid over into bed pulling the sheet over them. His huge hands were on her body now, one on the side of her encouraging her to slide down in the bed, the other between her moist tumid thighs separating the mounds of flesh, his hand trying to find a home in the heat between her legs. Pulling her slip up he started to caress her belly with his tongue, one hand still exploring the area between her thighs, the other gently kneading her breasts, as his tongue and now his lips pulled sucking the endless flesh of her belly. He went down in the bed turning on his stomach, pulling her down, both hands now rubbing her thighs, her hips, moving and kneading her stomach, thighs. Lightly licking the insides of her legs, her calves, his hand pushing, gently parting her thighs, inching up to the deep heat till his tongue found the pink opening between her legs and danced in her vagina till he found her clitoris. He stroked it gently, persistently, holding tight to her huge hips, her violent exhalations of breath exciting him as her large soft body began to rock, pitching forward and back as she uttered deep incoherent sounds. She was shaking now, covered with sweat, vibrating on the bed like a red and brown fish hollering ooh ooh as she went into uncontrollable spasms. He kept manipulating her clitoris with his tongue while she came. It was doing its own high red dance now as its owner shivered shaking tears from her eyes.

He rolled over on his back pulled off his shorts and dropped them gently on the floor beside the bed. He moved himself closer to the head of the bed and pulled the red slip the rest of the way over her head. He started to caress her face, freed her hair from the rubber band. He lifted himself on top of her, up down, his penis gently probing between her legs till his body found home, thrusting hard then soft, her holding onto him, him laid out on her, kissing each other, one hand exploring her body still; her own hands, one on his shoulder, the other on his buttocks. She was feeling over full now, like a volcano, aware and afraid of her own heat. She pulled him to her like a suction tube absorbing him in her mass, the heat, his, hers, fusing them together as he thrust into her again and again, his body shaking, her holding him as he exploded into little pieces inside of her. Mr. Henry was very still now, his big body beside hers, two different shiny browns glowing, quiet and still beside each other.

MR. HENRY LAY quietly while the sun came through the Venetian blinds like razors of light cutting across his chest. He watched Willa Mae hook her bra behind her back and pull on the ever-expanding panty hose that finally consumed her legs in their beige cocoon. His penis hardened as he remembered the heavy velvet of Willa Mae's breast falling on his chest, the damp ocean of her sex, the drugstore smell of her lotion and hair grease. Her magic was black, fat, like some holler in his genes, like the silence of sun over Georgia's red fields at noon. The room went dark suddenly. He looked up to see Willa Mae scowling, "Jus' a cloud passin'," she said reassuringly, "but it did look like rain for a minute." He wanted to grab her, pull off her white uniform, tear the ugly beige panty hose from her body, slam into her, ride her like a black road to the sky. But she had to go to work. He reached under the bed and pulled out a half-pint bottle and put it to his mouth.

He could not explain what he did next. The why of it. The invisible noise of the long walk he took when Willa Mae's lotioned body disappeared heavily out the door. The alcohol could not still the *why* sawing back and forth like metal teeth through his brain. He didn't even *like* Jadine, he thought disgustedly.

Down the hall Jadine lay quietly in bed listening to the hardwood floor creak under Willa Mae's bulk as she disappeared out the door to work. Jadine's breath was a thin bird caught in her throat that bolted out in little wet gasps as the floor boards began to creak again, this time under Mr. Henry's massive frame creeping down the hall to her room. Her breath flew out into the silence of his big black chest, dropping on her like an elevator carrying her down as his penis rolled like a black train in her vagina, her second mouth, opening, singing sweetly like the child she had been the first time. "Oh," she gasped. "in, *in*, harder Mr. Henry, it feels so good." The Stygian light eating up emptiness, exploding the darkness in her clitoris, sending wild light like animal tongues all over her body, licking. He thrust harder. Yes! she screamed against emptiness, deeper harder, please please Mr. Henry, in, in, *in*. She buckled under the pain of so much light, her legs snapped around him like rubber bands. She was full. Wheee! Jadine's little high-pitched voice soared up into the light, then stopped confused, flapped eerily for a second then crashed into a sad dark sound like a conductor calling out last stop in the middle of nowhere.

"Mr. Henry!" Willa Mae's voice broke every beam of light in the room when she screamed. She stood for a moment, frozen in the doorway. Then she moved, crashing a shopping bag of canned goods down on his face. Blood spurted from his cheek. She brought the bag down again. It seemed she would explode but she snorted and hurled her arsenal of canned peaches and beans to the floor and charged out of the room. Steel glinted above her head in her hand when she reappeared. Her eyes fell like tears over Jadine's body, the firm breasts and buttocks like dark bitter plums. The knife seemed frozen in the air, her hand unable to move it. "Get out!" she bellowed. Jadine and Mr. Henry appeared as frozen as her hand in the air. "Go!" she bleated, a sob wrenched from her propelling her like a big walrus toward Jadine, her arm, unfrozen, descending through the air. Jadine shrieked, her bladder emptied involuntarily as she bolted out the door like a terrified cat, naked, black, screeching, dribbling piss. Mr. Henry ran behind her.

WILLA MAE SAT down at the table and carefully placed some butter in the middle of the steaming pile of grits. The steaming whiteness and yellow so different from Mr. Henry's brown and Jadine's black. She shook her head, trying to force Jadine's shiny black legs out of her mind as she mashed her grits and eggs together with her fork, gently sprinkling the mixture with salt and pepper. She buttered a biscuit. Well, she was gone now, she thought, placing the golden edge of the biscuit in her mouth, following it with a bite of sausage. She ate slowly, deliberately, the thoughts which had been slicing through her like knives stopped and the world again became something to observe, serve, consume and bear. For a minute the methodical movement of her hand from her plate to her mouth stopped, and the yellow and white of the grits and eggs disappeared into the black and brown of Mr. Henry and Jadine. She shoulda killed him! Wish something had been boiling, wish Jadine had been cooking and left something on the stove. Grits, preferably. Bastard! She stood up, taking the five little sausages that were left in the pan and placing them carefully on her plate.

She chewed slowly, concentrating on the bland taste of the grits, the oily comfort of the butter; soon there was no sound but her fork scraping the plate, no colors but yellow and white and the golden brown of the biscuits. She really oughtta call Mrs. Goldstein and tell her she wouldn't be in tomorrow. She really did have to tend to her own house now. Willa Mae sighed, what was she gonna do with all Jadine's stuff? Her fork was poised in the air when she remembered there was always the Good Will. She should call Mrs. Goldstein now, she really should, she thought, putting the last of the crispy brown sausages in her mouth.

It was dark outside when Willa Mae Justice in a white uniform spattered with blood called her employer and told her she would not be in in the morning, nor the next day neither.

"I got somethings here I gotta take care of," Willa Mae said. Mrs. Goldstein listened attentively. Willa Mae did not get paid for sick days and in ten years had not missed a day of work.

"Well, Willie, what happened! Is Jadine alright? Are *you* alright?"

"I don't know how Jadine is and I'm alright. I just got some things to do."

"I mean . . . I . . . it's so . . . not like you, but O.K. I'll see you Monday."

"O.K. Mrs. Goldstein."

"You're sure, Willie? I can get Charles to help you, he's District Attorney now. If Jadine has gotten into some trouble—" she trailed off.

"I'm sure, ma'am," Willa Mae said with finality.

Willa Mae put the phone down and went into the kitchen and got two huge trash bags from under the sink. She walked to Jadine's room and stood in the doorway, looking. Books, bicycle, records, record player—all these years she'd never had a record player. She'd keep the record player, books, too. The bicycle, she couldn't do nuthin' with that, or them pictures of that long-haired nigger from Jamaica. Somebody could use the bicycle, though, mattress, too. Willa Mae ripped the dirty sheets from the bed, throwing them along with the blankets and bedspread into the plastic trash bag. She picked up the little wastebasket, threw it and its contents into the bag. Willa Mae began to tote the milk crates full of books one by one to the hallway near the front door, lining them neatly along the wall. She did the same with the records. If Jadine came for 'em they would be there, if not Willa Mae'd listen to 'em herself. Sweating, she touched the underarms of her uniform, looked down and became aware of blood splattered on it. Standing in the hallway she took the uniform off and dropped it on the floor. Her slip, brassiere, girdle, stockings and drawers followed. Covered with sweat, flesh peeking out the hole in her raincoat, her boots unzipped and flopping around her ankles—Willa Mae Justice was mounting the stairs to her apartment as Wakefield Green, the building super-intendent, was descending the stairs from his apart-ment on the fourth floor. He looked in disbelief. Willa Mae drunk? No, not in all the years he'd known her.

"Willa Mae," he said in the voice Jadine called sour, "you alright?"

"I'm fine, Mr. Green, jus' fine. What you up to?"

Now that he was up on her she didn't look drunk, just kinda wild and tired. "Well, I gotta put the trash out. What you doing?" He looked at her bare legs. She sighed, looking at his big scaly hands, dirty overalls and beat-up shoes.

"I was jus' cleanin' up, thas all, jus' cleanin' up," she replied. He was about to pass her on his way down when she turned to him and said, "I need some paint, Mr. Green."

"Some paint?" he echoed.

"Yeah, I got these walls Jadine painted, well I painted 'em. Jadine wanted 'em painted and I painted 'em for her. Lavender, they's lavender."

"Well you needs primer. Put dat on the wall, let it dry, paint on top of it and you'll be able to cover that lavender up with one coat."

"Alright, Mr. Hen-, I mean Mr. Green, what you got?"

"Well I got a green, real pale like, and I got gray—"

"No gray, Mr. Green."

"Well, I gots a real purty pink, almost white but its warm-like, creamy, a little like the color when the sun come up."

"Now that sounds real nice, Mr. Green."

"Willa Mae, jus' call me Wakefield, hear."

"O.K., Wakefield, that pink sounds real nice and I still got that gold trim left over from when I painted the last time."

"I'll bring the paint up soons I finish in the basement and outside, O.K.?"

"O.K., Wakefield."

Willa Mae emptied Jadine's dresser drawers into a second trash bag, along with her shoes, jewelry, vibrator; she'd stopped a second at the vibrator. Wonder what they did your hand couldn't. She threw Jadine's address book, little scraps of paper from on top the dresser, dirty panties, jeans, tiny lace bras, sweaters, t-shirts and socks into the bag. She hauled it to the closet near the front door. Willa Mae hauled the rug, then the dresser downstairs, then came back perspiring, standing in the doorway of Jadine's empty room, staring, trying to figure out what to do next.

She went and got her bucket, rags, Pinesol and broom. She swept, tackled the door, closet and plate around the light switch, then got down on her hands and knees to wash the baseboards and floor. She was through when Wakefield knocked on the door with three cans of paint. When she asked for a ladder he asked quite humbly if he could paint the ceiling and a foot down for her.

"I want that there," she pointed to the decorative plaster trim that ran around the wall a foot or so down from the ceiling, "done up in gold."

He nodded, "Well, O.K. Willa Mae, that ain't no problem." And it wasn't. Together they had the room glowing quiet pale pink and gold by daybreak.

Willa Mae was scrubbing the floor of what had been Jadine's room for the second time, the fumes of the drying paint around her head. In fact, at first she thought it was the paint fumes causing her to see colors in front her eyes, but it wasn't. She saw it clear as day, clear as *day*. The soft pale wall was lit up with the Star of Mississippi, what her grandmother had quilted, but it was a brighter star, a more vivid yellow set against a deeper blue and a red so sharp it was like a dog biting. Willa Mae bent down to put her rag back in the bucket and when she looked back up it was gone. It had been there, she assured herself as she finished scrubbing. It had been there.

She came back to the room after washing the dishes and scrubbing the kitchen and bathroom floors to pour salt in the corners of the room and set a bowl of water in the middle of the floor.

It was early, six or seven, when Willa Mae left her house to take a walk in the cool morning air. She was looking at the women standing at the bus stop with shopping bags full of uniforms and headache remedies when she saw her grandmother's full frame sifting through pieces of material. It was then Willa Mae knew she wasn't going back to Mrs. Goldstein. Wasn't nothin' to even think about. She'd find a way. She shook her head smiling while tears rolled down her cheeks. Willa Mae couldn't stop the thoughts or feelings now. She was thinking about Jadine, how she had felt when her tiny mouth was on her breast. The soft sweet flurry it sent through her body and how good it felt to be someone's sole source of nourishment, security and love; them coming from you, being you. It was the only feeling that had ever made her feel important. Willa Mae thought about the nickels, dimes and dollars that had bought Jadine's shoes, toothbrushes, coloring books and dolls and later things Jadine should have bought herself—diaphrams, dope and that poodle dog Jadine had starved. Willa Mae was crying, thinking about when Jadine had been eighteen and left home and how she had gone to get her, telling her she wasn't ready, when it was Willa Mae not ready. Well, I didn't know then like I know now, she mused. I just didn't know. Her mind turned to the scraps of brightly colored cloth in her closet and under her bed, the riot of colors, the possibilities. Well, you just be wrong sometimes, she concluded, wrong as two left shoes, but what's past is past, can't change the past. And tomorrow ain promised. But I got today, yeah, I got today and life to live. And I am.

Eat

"YOU TOO GOOD to eat my pussy?" she snorted.

I don't believe it, I thought.

Sunlight strained through deep purple velvet curtains, breaking through the white lace which was draped in front of the velvet. She sat at the head of the big comfortable bed surrounded by her dusty finery. Her body seemed like a series of alabaster poles wrapped loosely inside blue denim.

"Cough syrup?" she queried.

I nod.

"It's from China," she informs me. "High opium content."

"Really," I murmur. "I thought they weren't into that anymore."

"It's not from *that* China," she spit out.

"Oh, excuse me," I said apologetically.

Bob Dylan poured aquamarine and indigo from the stereo:

with your mercury mouth in the missionary times

"Did ya hear what I said?"

"Yeah, 'bout China."

"No," she said emphatically, "'bout eating my pussy."

Wow, this was deep. I wanted the cough syrup, but I wasn't gonna fuck for it.

"Here," she shoves me a dark amber bottle in a crumpled paper bag. I hand her a twenty. I look down at my string bag on the floor, filled with bread, cheese, and sweet, gold-flecked green grapes. The sounds of the street seep in through the window. I'd forgotten about Fontaine the six years I'd been away. Now, the week after my aunt's funeral, I'd found myself walking from one end of the city to the other. My feet had stopped in front of the old hotel remembering what I'd forgotten: the music, Jimi, Janis, Buddy Miles, water pipes, syringes, acid and strawberry incense, and Fontaine. I couldn't imagine she still lived here. I couldn't imagine her living anyplace else, though, I thought as my feet padded across the faded maroon carpet, my nose taking in the odor of old wood, perspiration, and cigarette smoke.

"Miss Fontaine, please, room 522," I had asked the faded little man behind the desk.

"Go right up," his voice limped softly.

It had seemed like years now since I had stepped out

of the elevator. Fontaine, gaunt and emaciated, stared at me with hard eyes. I reached for my bag.

"You just got here!" she wailed.

Dylan crooned:

with your sheets like metal and your belt like lace
and your deck of cards missing the jack and the ace

She was dying and I was leaving as fast as I could get up and get out of there. But I didn't go. I sat there staring at her quilt—astrological symbols of blue velvet squares juxtaposed with red roses on yellow squares. I looked at her shiny black leather riding boots. She looked at me looking.

"Brand new," she shrugged gesturing to the boots. "Never wore 'em before."

My knees felt like they had rusted but somehow I got up. I moved away from the curtains, fighting the light, away from the red roses on their yellow squares. The door was not far. I would get there.

Sad-eyed lady of the lowlands
where the sad-eyed prophet says that no man comes

I look back at Neptune on blue velvet and her long white arms coming out of her denim jacket.

Against the deep purple drapes she is whiter than the white lace.

Oh sad-eyed lady, should I wait?

Bones are revealed in stark relief as she strips away her clothes. Her body is an elongated tear. I am standing. My feet move, but not where I tell them. I am kneeling beside her now, helping her slide the hard boots off her feet, one, then the other. Now, the jeans. I gasp at the cavern between the two pale flares of her pubic bones.

I pull her pants off, dropping them beside the bed. Her arm goes around my neck like a hook.

"Wait," I plead. Her smell is harsh—fear, nicotine, perfume. No heat, no sex odor.

My breasts drop from my bra, warm with the heat of my body. Opening my jeans I am aware of the roundness of my brown belly as I slide my pants down. Dropping my pants on the floor next to hers I pull back the quilt, pull up the wrinkled sheet, and slide under the covers like a little girl. My hand on her arm tells her to do the same. Her eyes are silent beggars. I pull her on top of me. She seeps into me like sand. My hands move slowly over the psychic battlefield that is her body, over the war she is losing. Sadness fills me. My hand spans her thigh, her buttocks. Hold her, hold her, *hold her*, my soul screams. And it feels so good to hold someone I stop being horrified at what she has lost and marvel at what she has—life, breath, her legs between my opening thighs.

"Turn over," I whisper. Prayerfully my hands begin to move over her body like the wind, everywhere, finding armpit, shoulder, neck, lips, thighs, knees, breasts, stomach, buttocks, eyebrows, hair. I am putting a shell to my ear, trying to hear the sea. She begins to talk like the sea does, in whispers, moans, churnings. I move down in the bed and pull her vagina to my mouth. My tongue searching for life between her legs. One orifice pressed to another, to suck. First thing we know to do when we are born, suck—or die. My tongue beats her clitoris, joy spreading over my face as the sea begins to flow in my mouth.

"Please," she whispers.

I keep on, my mouth a warrior in a pink battlefield pushing back death. Feel, feel, *feel*, I will. Her body begins to rock in the old-time rhythm, and I know it won't be long. I keep on and on, her body mine, mine hers. I feel the soft moans coming from her throat before I hear them. My will is transformed to power. I pull her on top of me and we press our bodies together, rocking like Naomi and Ruth musta rocked. She pulls my head back down between her legs, the taste is alive in my mouth. She comes again and again. We hold each other quiet, long. She laughs like a warm soft bird in my arms. Stroking my face she whispers, "Momi, what can I do for you?"

I hesitate for a second, then reach for the string bag on the floor, pull out the sweet grapes. Holding them to her mouth I say, "Eat."

Arisa

4/23/86   9:50 A.M.
Weatherman had said mostly sunny but it's snowing today.
Arisa committed suicide yesterday.

10:30 A.M.
Her father said she was the most peaceful he had ever seen her. She jumped from the fourteenth floor, out the back window. The maintenance man found her. She died with her eyes open.

All the envy and hate between us, my intense jealousy of her body, her overdeveloped calves and slender thighs, she was on my mind often, an irritant. I thought earlier of a line from a play, "Love is not the only tie that binds," and how that little buck-toothed Arisa had my mind. I always wanted to hurt her. I always thought if she came here I would not let her come in. I remember she told Anita, her lover, she didn't like me and C.M. because we were vicious.

I remember when I was doing choreography for Edwina, and Arisa went OFF talking about how the steps couldn't be done in that timing and finally how she stamped out of the room saying she couldn't do the piece. Then she turned around and did the very step I'd put together in her solo! Edwina had to tell her you just can't do that. Later she would tell Anita I tried to steal her Brazilian steps.

I remember the time looking at a picture of me she said, "They just don't know how beautiful you are." Yesterday I thought of her. She can dance, but she's still ugly, that's what I thought. I had heard her on WBAI, the Lesbian Show, talking to Judy Pasternack. I didn't know who she was then. I remembered her voice. Arisa said, you gotta go back to that little girl and give her the love she didn't get. But on the radio I don't really remember what it was she talked about. Said she lived with her father and danced, Lester Horton technique. Judy did Horton, too. A black man called up after Arisa spoke and said as a white person Judy couldn't speak for a black woman. Judy said he couldn't speak for a black woman as a man.

"To show you how much of a feminist I was," Arisa said, introducing herself at Salsa's cultural affair, "I usta be a Playboy Bunny." She said she had read my work in a third world lesbian magazine, said it was the only good thing in the magazine or the best thing, I forget which. I had nothing for her. I wanted to be *real*, reflect the *real* feelings between us: I don't like you and you don't like me, so let's stop bullshitting. But for awhile I dreamed of Arisa constantly. Had to admit she wasn't ugly. The colors she wore—turquoise, lavender, those yellow overalls—I wanted to wear. My eyes would be on her. I was attracted to her. She thought everyone was in love with her. Said R. was attracted to her. I told her I wanted to put my poetry together and perform it. She said, I think you could.

I envied her confidence, assertion, acceptable body. She seemed to believe in herself. Believing seemed to have made her beautiful. All her beautiful clothes! I felt tacky in comparison. In *comparison*. She was always in competition. "I was the best," she said when we came back from Europe on tour. Well ok, now what bitch? You were the best. I don't even know if she really believed that. She beat me on the ground that didn't belong to either of us. By *their* standard, the one that drove her crazy and out the window. She died with her eyes open. We were never friends and I didn't like her.

I've never known it to snow so late.

1:50 P.M.
Arisa was a lesbian, a witch, and an Aries.

4/29/86   4:05 A.M.
sleep is over me
like a dark cloud
my throat is raw tight
my mouth sour salty
robbed of dreams
coming from the underground
I awake.

I'm tired already
of cleaning
this white bitch's house,
her white body
clad in black.
IRT line brings
me down from
Harlem to clean today.
I worry when
I'm gone,
3 locks
I leave
the radio
& lights on
still I worry
they'll get in.
I try to think positive
in circles of shimmering
white light;
everything is white
down here on the upper west side,
you are over it all

invisible
does anybody
see me?
I hope not,
pushing this
baby carriage
4:15 o'clock
in the morning
sour fuzzy shit
lives in your mouth.
you have gone
thru this
before,
it's all
frightfully hard,
you wish
you were dancing
on long legs in Paris,
but you're not.
J. says Arisa
was mentally ill
& we don't know what
that's really like.
I know that
she fell
flying.
Arisa's jumps
were always
good.
up until
this last one

I felt she lacked
a sense of drama,
the ability
to express herself
fully,
but she did
just fine
this time.
my pen stops
at the bruise on
the side of her face,
and how old she looked
in that casket,
jaw clenched
lips pieced like clay
and pressed together
over her large teeth,
that white dress
folded hands waxen.
your father says
he never saw you
so peaceful,
he was probably
tired of you
too.
you were a
hard one to get
anything
out of
and always angry.
sometimes

I saw breath
fill your body
& turn you
soft cloud
turquoise blue,
rest
sigh
you hated
me too.
you knew
what was wrong
with everyone
except yourself.
now you
are gone,
you who never
really had to
work for a living,
fine tuned
cellulite-free
burning bright
stumbling
silly
pitiful
admirable
strong
courageous
Arisa,
who never wore
the rubber gloves
of defeat.

I can't guarantee
how,
but that you'll
be remembered
is sure,
as I trudge thru
white ladies' houses
without style
or dreams,
things you never
had to do,
I'll remember
your horrible
brilliant smile,
how strong &

beautiful
your legs
&
ahh yes—
how well
you
jumped.

Violet '86

1.

The brown velvet doll has beads for eyes, long braids of real hair and cowrie shells for lips. The first doll I ever made. I call her Little Africa, L.A. for short. You won't take her. You're afraid someone in the hospital will steal her, or that the hospital staff won't let you keep her.

I finger the necklace I've taken from your house. Admonish myself. You are not dead yet. Fingering the round purple beads I think of your house full of purple towels, knickknacks, yarn.

"Why purple, Mommy?" I ask. "Why purple?"

You say, "For passion, love." You say the doll is

beautiful, adorable, but you won't take her. I tell you I made her, tell you, "I'm not angry anymore."

You wave your hand at my need to say what you already know.

"I love you."

"I know," you say. "I love you, too."

I pick the doll up and make her dance, bouncing her up and down on your bed. I am singing and dancing as I make the doll dance. I hold the doll up, she says, "I love you," with her cowrie shell mouth, her asymmetrical legs bouncing in the air.

"I love you, too," you answer.

I put the doll away, stand to leave. "I just came to say good-bye."

You look so sad and little and brown.

"Don't say good-bye," you say, "just say 'so long.'"

2.

The nurse beckons to me as I approach your door. She tells me you have pulled off your oxygen mask and barricaded yourself in the bathroom to smoke a cigarette. You feel everyone is against you. I want to know, are you crazy or suffering from oxygen deprivation.

Forewarned, I peek my head around the door. You turn to me like a little hurt bird. You are glad to see me. The nurse and I exchange glances of relief. I am not part of the plot against you. But what am I supposed to say? Shit, finally you know what's happening. Everyone *is* against you, except me and Dr. Staddon. Dr. Staddon has a program where you could die with some peace and dignity. Everyone else wants you to take the chemo. You can't breathe. One lung is collapsed. The pneumonia is a particularly virulent kind. The pneumonia compounds the leukemia, the leukemia the pneumonia. A catheter would be inserted into your aorta, the poison would be pumped into your body. It would immediately kill off the leukemia cells, and you. *And you* is what they neglect to tell you. But you know, deep inside you know.

The next day I walk into your room. A monster is sitting on your bed. His face is covered with white gauze. He is dressed in thin sick-blue paper pants and coat. On his head is a shower cap, white plastic bags cover his shoes. He is coarse, red and ugly. He is rich. He is white. He is the surgeon come to get you to sign papers to pump poison into your aorta. I am poor. I am black. I am a woman. I run to you. His gloved hand moves toward the papers, but my hand is upon them first. I face the devil with no deodorant or degrees.

"What are the possible dangers of this type of surgery?"

"Well, of course," he says as if he is addressing a mosquito, "infection, lung collapse—"

"Lung collapse!"

"Well, the catheter could possibly puncture the lung when it's being inserted—"

"Which lung?"

"*Which* lung?" he echoes.

"Well, one lung is already collapsed as a result of the pneumonia."

"Oh, of course, then we would, ahh, insert it over the other lung."

"Which is?"

"Well I don't know all that—"

"How will the operation itself affect her pneumonia since she already has trouble breathing?"

"I can't answer that," he snaps, "I just put the catheter in. I'm the surgeon."

"He doesn't know if this will be in your best interest," I say slowly. "You don't have to do this. It's to his economic advantage to perform as many operations as possible. I don't think this is a good idea."

You pat my black hand. Already my veins protrude like yours. You hand the papers to the doctor and tell me, "You shouldn't have come. The doctors know, and your brother thinks this is best."

"When?" I ask realizing you have already signed the papers.

"In a few days."

"*When?*"

"A week from now, Wednesday."

I look at you, broken, brown and dying. I try to tell myself maybe. Maybe you can stand the onslaught. Maybe you know something I don't. Maybe a miracle.

Two days after the tube you are dead.

3.

The business of death takes away feeling, gives detachment. Everywhere my hands perform this last prayer, folding, stacking, discarding, cleaning. Bag after bag of trash hauled in the heat, scrubbing a filthy toilet seat, scraping mold out of dishes, dusting, determining, separating, saving. What is to be saved after sixty-five years? What is trash and what is valuable?

I take your sewing machine, the purple vases that graced your window, the sewing kit, Bible, watches, leather gloves, perfume, pictures and letters.

I clean and clean. Finally there is a stack in front of your dresser four feet high. Your sister can sort through these things. I couldn't find the one picture I wanted. And letters, I feel there were more. The house is clean and orderly. No one will come in here thinking you were a crazy, dirty old lady. Your bedside is neat and elegant. I leave incense burning in an iridescent mauve ashtray, one of the last things you made. It says "Violet '86" underneath. A radical departure in color and style from the work of twenty years ago that says, "Lofton." I leave lavender towels hanging, the refrigerator clean, the plants watered. I draw the curtains, light a candle. Aretha Franklin drifts poignant and haunting from an ancient record player: *hey baby let's get away . . . someplace far . . .*

I've cleared off the tables that were stacked with magazines and dirty ashtrays. All over, you had crystal bowls filled with matches and candy. These are washed out and emptied. I stare at the bottle in my hand: Pure Pac p solution 1% Gentian Violet (aqueous). I fill the bowls with water, flick drops of the deep purple solution into the bowls. Slowly the deep dark drops expand turning the water a wonderful clear purple color. The house is sweet-smelling and peaceful. I turn off Aretha and stand looking over where you used to live. You wanted me to bring my friends, to meet them. I never did. Too much water under the bridge, I thought then, to play mother and daughter. But I stand here now dusty and tired in my daughter's duty. You are gone now, all possibilities closed like the coffin over your face. We have no tomorrows, you and I, only a past and places in my dreams. I whisper hesitantly, on my way out the door, "Come on back and see me if you can."

AUTOPSY REPORT 86–13504

1.   the coroner could
have been your lover
or a poet
how he described you
little razor knife cutting
to blurred type
on stapled pages—
Michael(you had hell learning to spell that name,
stuttering up to M-I-C-H, not knowing whether the
'a' or 'e' came next)*Lofton.*

I hold a 9 by 12 manilla envelope that contains your
birth certificate, death certificate & autopsy report.
was prophylactic used in baby's eyes?
yes
if yes, state drug
AgN03.
serological test for syphilis made in this mother?
yes
to this mother children previously born?
none.
place of death: park
hour: 0745
air temperature: 74
3 children skating fall backward thru an emerald sun
remains found supine on ping pong table in the park.
the grass bleeds & the wind spells correctly:
M-I-C-H-A-E-L.

2.   when you were born it said: Negro
now you are dead it says: Black
BLACK
BLACK
we have made progress?
you were the first one who told me
there was no place called NERGO LAND.
staring at the death certificate
i realize you've tricked me again
like when we were teenagers & you'd
promise to take me partying with you & Hartley,
would tell me, "hurry up and get dressed" and
while i was changing clothes you'd leave me . . .

3.   *Autopsy Report 86–13504*
From the anatomic findings and pertinent history
I ascribe death to craniocerebral injuries
Los Angeles, Ca. October 14, 1986, @ 1230 hours
subcutaneous
subgaleal
subdural
cerebral
cerebellar
extensive
skull
fractures
the body is that of a well-developed black male
74 inches in length
tall
weighing 179 pounds

appearing the stated 38 years of age
37! he was 37!
the hair is long
measuring 6 inches in length
in an afro style.
there is also a moustache
& slight beard growth
the sclerae are white
& the irises are brown.
nose shows blood
the left ear contains blood & fly eggs.
the mouth shows fly eggs on the hard palate
the teeth appear to be intact
thorax symmetrical
configuration normal abdomen flat
you
extremities show no
were
clubbing, edema or deformity
beautiful
the external genitalia are those
of a normal circumcised adult male
skin free of tattoos, tumors or needle marks:
blood in the throat is smooth and glistening
dark red
scattered diffusely
normal coronary pattern
branching
yes
yes
like a tree

running smooth &
free
no thromboses
or clogged arteries
lumina wide patent
free
what went wrong?
the pleural surfaces show scattered subpleural
hemorrhages
foci of parenchyma show apparent aspiration
of blood.

4.   right
left
extensive
Head and Nervous System
damage
soul
contorted
locked
up
busted
penitentiary.
you said it was fuck
or be fucked.
said they let you out
with a string attached to
your ass to pull you back
if you breathe wrong.

Lord Lofton
number 7!

conquer of light
mystical magic
mumbo jumbo
thighs flashing
down Hollywood Blvd,
canvassing Watts, Compton, the jungle.
mighty Leo
hunter without a game
hurt brown lion
roar choked quiet.
postal employee, cab driver, bank robber, but
that's all worlds behind you now
as you wander talking to trees
in the land of tin dreams.
reduced to rubble
LORD LOFTON
King of Nothing.

5.   Sapphire,

I sent a letter up to the other address explaining
the times and change of life. Since the happenings of
the last letter things look better being that I remember
where I was a year ago (in jail). Also walking down
Sunset to get my last check from the big 'Z' I happen
to look behind me and see this sister and white boy
walking together. She looked as if she didn't want to be
bothered, so I gave her the high sign and she ducked
into a phone booth and I into a store. She came out
and we started walking down the street arm and arm
exchanging words no names yet.

She told me she had a friend around the corner
with some jam, so we walked by and got Hi. Found out
later she is S— S— of Earth, Wind and Fire. Spent
last night at her apartment on Sunset. Saph for the
record I have never been so Hi! in my life and awake
to remember it: wine, coke, hash and opium. Yes, once
again I am in love chasing the happiness (so called)
that we all chase.

Other than that money is getting funny.
Power to Us
Lord Lofton

6.   marijuana bust fires you from the post office
job driving cab loses you.
soon you see nothing,
you are the 'Crenshaw Bandit'
debonair thief,
'7 banks with his wits'
they can't put their finger on you
invisible in $500 shoes,
magic mushroom & plum wine
aboard a rented jet listening to Pink Floyd
dancing under rose-colored lights
on Century Blvd with onyx women
till cold bone steel saws you in two.

you say it's not the time but the time afterwards—
petty busts
stretching parole 8 years
harassment, burning asphalt
& you, the lion, convinced he has no heart

follow road
after yellow road
back to your father's house.
the house he did not
want you in,
where daily he told you
you were nothing
nobody,
pull yourself together
get a job
take a bath
mow the lawn
leave that dope alone
get outta here boy.

oppressed white bitch has you locked up when you go OFF in the parole office hollerin' bout you're a BLACK MAN & she can't tell you nothin! her power-starved eyes look at your delicate veined black strength & throw you in a loony bin just to show you what she can do.

7.   Sapphire,
     7:00 P.M. Sunday eating stale bread and butter, lunch and dinner. It has been a week. I had a '71 Eldorado, a white prostitute, been put in jail, had Sylvia and Miss Watkins get me out and put the white ho in jail, lost 10 pounds, spent a day with Little Brother, showed him Hollywood, partied, introduced him to S— S— and closed out the week at the 'So What Club' on Vermont and Jefferson with Iceberg

Slim, the Pimp.
   David said hello and that he is finishing your
   picture.
   May be up there in S.F. the first, don't know.
   Don't know if I'll be here tomorrow.
   Ready to move, phone off, gas off,
   waiting for the door bell to ring, what is next
      LORD LOFTON
      must hustle the eight cent for the stamp now

8.   the park was green.
we usta hide in the bushes
waiting for my father's old green & white Ford
to pass by on his way to work
so we could turn around & go back
home
away from school,
the world.
at school, a button strained
to breaking at her bulging middle,
a stringy-haired white
teacher tells me,
the only difference between
the jews & black people is
black people haven't been
wiped out yet.
I go OFF
& a classroom full of hip black kids
who can do things I can't—sing, dance, fight,
who used to intimidate me & command my
respect sit in silence,

they are silent.
my father, 'the old fool,' we call him
tells me to obey the teacher
mind the rules, keep my mouth
shut, learn something—
he has no balls
or brains
or heart
but he has the house
the house he puts us out of
the house with the chain on the
refrigerator, plastic on the couch,
rose bushes & rubber hose.
the house with the two-car garage
he puts the disassembled pieces
of your bed in.

9.   Sapphire,
     Things have gotten worse.
     Write to the old fool's. Going to take most of the
stuff there and hit the road of L.A.
     I did some business with Carol and have not seen
money or her. On the coke side. Have the 3 day
notice to pay or quit my pad.
     May be on the way north. Too many things are
crowding down on me.
     Michael

10.   time passes like blood
pumping thru your veins.

you weren't interested in my poems,
resented how throughly i'd escaped—

New York, the Big Apple
i can't eat
i can't sleep
10 years i am here
the blood pumps thru
my heart warm
as yours is cold.

11.   Sapphire,
        . . . her name is Mercy and she has a Triumph
    and she likes me . . . cute, well to do, party, young
    freak. Should be an interesting summer. Wonder
    why you wouldn't answer any of the letters sent to
    you . . .
        One goal, I would like a Jaguar and Paris, the
    city . . . if nothing underforeseen hits have your
    number will call with the late and the latest.
        Lord Lofton

12.   fracture lines extend anteriorly
on the left wing
of the sphenoid
orbiting extensively along
the temporal bone
to the petrous ridge.
representative sections
of all major organs
are taken for the hold jar.
hair long

sex male
race black
no tracks
teeth intact
tall
samples of heart blood and urine are saved.

opinion: This 38-year-old black male died as a result of
  multiple blows . . .

13.   . . . Bye for now,
    Love Michael
    LORD LOFTON

where jimi is

go now.
I used to follow you
you never could get rid of me.
now since you're dead
it's you
following me,
trying to escape that last exit—
the obsessive smelly
wet lips of death.
go now,
this is too long to wander.
1986 was your time.

go now.
it's not a devouring
void forever
black.
it's not gonna be like that, Michael
i promise.
death is where
jimi hendrix is,
where our revolution
ended up.
death—why mommy's there
and she has time
for you
now.

There's a Window

"IS THIS JUST something to do till you get out? Till you get back to your old man?" she sneered.

I didn't answer her. I just kept pushing her blue denim smock further up her hips. The dress was up to her waist now. I wanted to get one of her watermelon-sized breasts in my mouth. I was having trouble with her bra.

"Take off your bra."

"Oh, you givin' orders now," she said, amused. Her short spiked crew cut and pug nose made her look like a bulldog. Her breath smelled like cigarettes, millions of 'em.

"Yeah," I asserted, "I'm giving orders. Take that mutherfuckin' harness off."

She laughed tough but brittle. The tough didn't scare me, the brittleness did. She nuzzled my ear with her nose, her hot, moist lips on my neck. "Call me Daddy," she whispered.

Oh no, I groaned. She stuck her tongue under my chin. It was like a snake on fire. Fuck it, I'd call her anything.

"O.K., Daddy," I sneered. "Take off your bra." Something went out of her. I felt ashamed. "I'm sorry," I whispered trying to put it back. I had the dress up over her waist now.

"Take it off," I whispered.

"My blues!" she protested, referring to the denim prison smock.

"Yeah, I don't wanna fuck no piece of denim. Take off that ugly ass dress." I was eating up her ear now. My tongue carousing behind her ear and down her neck that smelled like Ivory Soap and cigarette smoke. I was sitting on top of her belly pumping my thighs together sending blood to my clitoris as I pulled the dress over the top of her head. I was riding, like the Lone Ranger on top of Silver. No, take that back. Annie Oakley, I was riding like Annie Oakley. Actually, I should take that back, too, but I can't think of any black cowgirls right off hand. Looking down at her face I wanted to turn away from it, keep my eyes focused on the treasure behind the white cotton harness. Hawk-eyed, crew cut butch, she was old compared to me. How the fuck did she keep her underwear so clean in this dingy hole, I marveled. They acted like showers and changes of clothes were privileges. I leaned down stuck

103

my tongue in her mouth realized in a flash the Ivory Soap clean bra and perspiration breaking out on her forehead was all for me.

She was trying. Trying hard. Probably being flat on her back with me on top of her was one of the hardest things she'd ever done. I admired her for a moment. Shit, she was beautiful! Laying up under me fifty years old, crew cut silver. I'd told her in the day room when she slammed on me, "Hey, baby, I don't want no one putting no bag over my head pulling no train on *me*. Shit, baby, if we get together it's got to be me doing the wild thing, too!"

She'd said, "Anything you want, Momi."

I slid down in the brown country of her body following blue veins like rivers; my tongue, a snake crawling through dark canyons, over strange hills, slowing down at weird markings and moles. I was lost in a world, brown, round, smelling like cigarette smoke, pussy and Ivory Soap. My hands were on her ass pulling her cunt closer to my mouth.

"Here," she said pushing something thin slippery and cool into my hand. I recognized the feel of latex.

"Just to be on the safe side," she said.

My heart swelled up big-time inside my chest. Here we was in death's asshole, two bitches behind bars, hard as nails and twice as ugly—caring. She *cared* about me, she cared about herself. I stretched the latex carefully over her wet opening. "Hold it," I instructed while I pulled her ass down to my mouth. I started to suck; that latex might keep me from tasting but it couldn't keep me from feeling. And I was a river now, overflowing its banks, rushing all over the brown mountains. I was a black cowgirl, my tongue was a six shooter and my fingers were guns. I was headed for the canyon, nobody could catch me. I was wild. I was bad.

"Oh, Momi," she screamed.

Um huh, that's me, keep calling my name. I felt like lightning cutting through the sky. She pulled me up beside her. I stuck my thigh between her legs and we rode till the cold cement walls turned to the midnight sky and stars glowing like the eyes of Isis. The hooves of our horses sped across the desert sand, rattlesnakes took wings and flew by our side. The moon bent down and whispered, "Call me Magdelina, Momi. Magdelina is my name."

Our tongues locked up inside themselves like bitches who were doin' life. No one existed but us. But the whispering moon was a memory that threatened to kill me. She slid down grabbing my thighs with her big calloused hands.

"Yeah, yeah, yeah," the words jumped out my throat like little rabbits. "Go down on me go down on me." Her tongue was in my navel. "Use dat latex shit," I told her.

"Do I have to, mamasita?"

"Yeah," I said, "I like the feel of it." I lied. My heart got big size again. They didn't give nothin' away in this mutherfucker. How many candy bars or cigarettes had she traded for those little sheets of plastic?

"Ow!" Shit, it felt good her tongue jamming against my clitoris. Oh please woman don't stop I begged but at the same time in the middle of my crazy good feeling something was creeping. I tried to ignore it and concentrate on the rivers of pleasure she was sending through my body and the pain good feel of her fingers in latex gloves up my asshole. But the feeling was creeping in my throat threatening to choke me. Nasty and ugly it moved up to my eyes and I started to cry. She looked at me concerned and amazed, "Mira Momi, did I do something wrong?" She glanced around, then at herself as if to assess where evil could have come from. "Not this damn thing?" she says incredulously. Her eyes gleam with the hope of alleviating my pain as she hastily unhooks her bra. I shake my head no no but she has her head down, her hands behind her back pulling the white whale off her brown body.

"I . . . I don' know, you know I have this *thing* about being totally naked—*here* you know. I ain't been naked in front of nobody since I been here, 'cept, you know, doctors and showers and shit," she laughed in her glass voice. "It jus' ain't that kind of place, mamasita. You know you snatch a piece here, there; push somebody's panties to the side in the john so you can finger fuck five minutes before a big voice comes shouting, 'What's takin' you so long in there!' Least that's what it's been like for me. Seven years," she said. The glass broke in her throat, "Seven years."

Her words overwhelmed me. I felt small and ashamed with my pain. But this thing in my throat had snatched my wings. I knew I had to speak my heart even though it felt juvenile and weak. Speak or forever be tied up to the ground.

"I ain't seen the moon or the stars in six months." I

felt ashamed—six months next to seven years on the edge of nothing. Silly shit to be tear-jerking about. I started to cry. I had seven years to do yet. She'd be gone by the time I turned around twice. She looked at me thoughtfully, her gray crew cut seemed like a luminous crown on top her forehead creased with lines. "Listen," she said quietly. "In six months or so you'll go from days in the laundry to the midnight to 8 A.M. kitchen shift if your behavior is good. Volunteer to peel the potatoes. There's a window over where they peel the vegetables. You can see the moon from that window."

I felt the nipples of her huge breasts hardening in my fingers. We retrieved two more precious pieces of latex, fitted ourselves in a mean sixty-nine and sucked each other back to the beginning of time. I was a cave girl riding a dinosaur across the steamy paleolithic terrain snatching trees with my teeth, shaking down the moon with my tongue.

poem for jennifer, marla, tawana & me

1.

she brought it on herself . . .
it was her own fault . . .
she did it to herself . . .

> Jennifer Levin was murdered by Robert Cham-
> bers in Central Park. His attorney said Ms.
> Levin had provoked her killer by violent sex
> play.

> Marla Hanson, a model, refused to relate sexu-
> ally to her landlord and demanded that he
> return her security deposit. He, a white man,
> responded by hiring a black man to slash her face
> with a straight razor. The black man's attorney
> asserted Marla Hanson was a racist.

> Tawana Brawley said she was abducted and raped
> by six white men. She was found in a trash bag
> smeared with dog shit, 'KKK' and 'nigger'
> scrawled on her chest. Because she had a boy-
> friend in jail, liked to party and had an allegedly
> abusive stepfather, it was insinuated she made the
> whole thing up to avoid being beaten by her
> parents.

i am thinking about the scratches on Robert Cham-
bers's face and hands. a witness would later testify he
looked like he'd been in an industrial accident. him

sitting across the road on a wall watching as her body
was discovered.

>   her sister said, "Robert Chambers killed her
>   once and the press killed her all over again a
>   second time."

Marla Hanson, Tawana Brawley and Jennifer Levin
>   twice victims
>   smeared and cut open
>   by *The Post*, *The Daily News* and *The New York
>   Times*

a woman must be a good girl, virgin, myth of a thing
in order to be raped. any other kind of woman brought
it on herself, did it to herself, it was her own fault, her
own fault . . .

2.

>   it was not her fault
>   it was not her fault
>   *it was not her fault*
>   it was not
>   it was not
>   it was *not*
>   he was not titillated into killing her
>   he was not provoked into killing her
>   he did not slash her face as a social
>   protest against racism
>   he slashed her face because he'd been
>   reduced to the level of protoplasm, alive
>   with no purpose but to smear hate and

defeat like feces on a child's body
Tawana
Tawana
Tawana
                    Lisa Steinberg
                    Lisa Steinberg
                    you did not talk too loud
                    wet the bed too much
                    there is nothing you did
                    it is not your karma
                    Myo ho ren ge kyo
                    the cause is sexism
                    the effect is murder, rape and child abuse

                    because you have a boyfriend in jail
                    because you are reactionary or even racist
                    because you like to fuck
                    is not just cause for the life
                    to be choked out of you
                    for a razor to slice your face
                    to the bone
women, it could be you traveling home from your
    boyfriend's apartment or jail cell
it could be you demanding your money back from a
    crooked landlord
it could be you wanting romance on a starry night in
    the park

i've been raped. i am afraid of that happening again.
what could i do but be silent?
the first question they ask will be about my past

and what could i say?
i *am* that type of girl.
it is documented and known i have been with
many many men for many many reasons.
how could *i* be raped?

3.

go back for the bones of the Hillside Strangler's victims
  those are my bones
  bleaching white
  under a California sun
  a teenager on the run
go back for the arms of that 15-year-old girl, hacked
 off, falling
  on a motel room floor
  her blood mingling with the blood
  of blind prostitutes in Hong Kong
  lined up in an alley full of fever
  and sightless eyes
go back for my bones, arms, eyes
  years ago i sat next to a white woman
  with blonde hair and she told me how
   6 black men
  picked her up, raped her, stuck a .38
  up her vagina and threatened to
  'shoot off' in her.
  i went home to write her story
  because she couldn't.
  but my pen froze on the page

i could not see clear to tell
the truth
because i wanted to protect
'the victims' who were her perpetrators.
but now my pen flows with the rage
from her blue eyes, the amputated scream of
    Tawana's
brown eyes and the blood of that 15-year-old
girl armless in California.
i have no one to protect but women,
let these men keep clutching their balls
crying about how hard it is to be a man.
just give me a wash cloth so i can wash
Tawana Brawley's face,
a pen so i can finally appease my goddess
who has been waiting 10 years
for me to write about the white woman
with blonde hair taken for a ride,
a gun shoved up her vagina.

my bones scatter the earth
my tears are the blood of too many women
my teeth fall out my mouth when i don't speak

i know my bones.
i could recognize them
anywhere!
and they're there
bleaching white
under a California sun.
the victims were poor women

the victims were black women
the victims were prostitutes
no one missed them
dogs discovered their
bones
bleaching
white
under the
sun

4.

what do you think about when death approaches?
i just remember scratching the side of my leg
while hands tightened around my throat as i slid
down the wall of my father's house into darkness.
my sister's scream loosened the hands around my neck
then there was air, light, life.
i don't even remember the guy's name,
he was just playing around he said,
wanted to see what it was like to choke someone,
didn't mean to hurt me, he said.
what could i say, do?
i wasn't supposed to be home anyway,
i was playing hookey from school,
i could hear my father's voice:

> what were you doing with a boy
> in the house?
> why weren't you in school?
> who is he?

why'd you let him in?
if you hadn't of . . .
if you hadn't of . . .
if you hadn't of . . .

as far as i know those fingers that squeezed my throat 25 years ago are still free, all the men who hurt me are still free, some are politicians now, famous singers . . .

my first boyfriend slapped my head like a ping-pong ball, hitting it back n forth, back n forth

could i tell my father? my father who also slapped my head like a ping-pong ball.

no, i couldn't tell him because in all the days of my life i have never seen my father or either of my brothers strike another man. never ever.

i remember my father saying 'yes suh,' 'no suh,' stressing the importance of dressing correctly, finishing school, keeping the house clean and disposing of sanitary napkins properly.

i knew he would not protect me and did not respect me. i was supposed to be grateful he didn't kill me.

if i had told the police about the fingers choking me? would the fact my father abused me invalidate my accusation?

because i fucked in cheap motels, back seats, bushes, beaches—

did i deserve to be bones?

5.

use my bones as spears—
whittle, carve, sharpen.
let them be knives thru the heart
or razors
severing testicles.
let them impale our killers
and gouge out their eyeballs.
and when the land bleeds clean of them,
use my bones to build a house
where we may heal
and unlearn the patriarchy.
a house where my father
cannot come, unless
he comes for forgiveness.

Human Torso Gives Birth

I MET HER in *Jet* magazine 10,000 years ago. The father of the baby preferred not to have his name known.

> eight to eighty
> blind, crippled or crazy
> a hard dick has no conscience
> (or embarrassment)
> men will stick their dick anywhere

I am not *anywhere*, she says. I am a person. It was a person he stuck his dick in. That hole between where legs shoulda been was not a cylindrical sphere of emptiness a falling pine knot left in a fence. I am not a hole in a fence. I was a woman that, those nights, all he wanted as I scooted over the sheets, my lips claiming his penis, my tongue his anus. He held my shoulders down and plunged into me like a tank rolling through town. I was a woman in a war zone, ravished and ready, surrounded by gun metal and singeing flesh.

Now he tells me it was a bad dream that made him ashamed.

But they can't take my baby from me. I won't let them she says determinedly. I am more fun than a circus as I show the judge how I can change a diaper with my teeth and tongue.

I dream of a bearded Japanese lover chasing me under the full moon. The moon is bleeding, my feet push off the sand and my legs are strong and swift. I hit the highway, blood pouring out the sky, my arms swinging as I run.

I dream of breaking bricks with my fists, turning flips and flying across the stage at Madison Square Garden. Black female sixth-degree black belt, all the people screaming and cheering me on.

She stops talking and fumbles with her tongue trying to push the Velcro tabs of the diaper together. I move to help her. Her face dies when she says thank you. I realize she has had to say thank you forever.

She sticks her tongue in the baby's navel. It laughs. She rubs her head against its cheek. Looking at me she says with the fervor of the sea, "Maybe my baby will be a samurai."

118

Questions for the Heart of Darkness

jungle prelude 1958

Sitting on the living room floor watching Saturday morn-
ing cartoons the sound of tom-tom drums envelops the black
child as a dark silhouette of the continent of Africa appears
on the screen than fades into an overhead view of tangled
vines and palm trees with huge fronds teeming with
monkeys and snakes. The picture drops down to a Stanley
Livingstone–type cartoon character with a big bushy mus-
tache wearing a safari hat. Bermuda shorts, knee socks and
hiking boots trekking up a jungle trail. On the side of the
trail in black spaces between the thick foliage you can see
pairs of big white eyeballs with beady black irises. The
eyeballs are following Livingstone up the trail. The tempo of

the tom-tom drums slows and a bunch of black African cartoon characters with bones through their noses and huge white lips like donuts spring out of the tangled underbrush. Wielding spears and grunting, they surround Stanley Livingstone, tie him up, hoist him over their shoulders and proceed up the trail. Barefoot and naked, except for grass skirts around their waists, they arrive (in about 2 seconds) at a clearing with a circle of grass huts from which many more black people erupt, with spear in their hands, shouting ooga ooga. The beating of the tom-tom drums mounts to a frenetic pitch. One of the blacks reaches down inside his scanty grass skirt and pulls out a salt shaker and all the blacks surge toward Stanley. Pulsating to the rhythms of the tom-toms, they move to a huge pot in the center of the grass huts; they put Stanley into the pot, shake salt on him, and light a fire under the pot. Then, lips grinning like a sea of white donuts, the blacks reach down under their skirts and pull out sparkling stainless steel knives and forks.

So where is this heart of darkness? On tv
in the 50s with a bone stuck through its nose?

Why don't these cartoons ever leave us Mr. ——?

You say you were just having fun,
that black people are too sensitive,
that the images were never meant to
destroy or demean?

Mr. ——, did you read the Sunday paper on
clean formica countertops eating eggs like

fried yellow eyes remembering dark fire?
Monday did you slide under mahogany tables in board-
rooms with enormous blonde secretaries, windows
   with a view
and men made of briefcases and penile implants and
   say:
Deposit the nuclear wastes in Zaire?

Do your daughters wake up sweating with nightmares
   of
black savages when all along it was you, Mr. ——,
over the green, under the pale horrible moon?
Are you a sheet wrapped around the blackest night
riding in a Cherokee jeep headlights bright blinding
   pulling
to the side of the moon, shoulder of the road, one
   minute after midnight?
Did you eat the black fire in your daughter's eyes?

Saturday morning over bowls of cornflakes floating
   like
gold boats in a white sea did your children laugh at
   cartoons
depicting indigenous African peoples as cannibals with
bones through their noses chasing white people
through the 'jungle' with spears?

Have we had to endure the burden of your
projection for centuries, Mr. ——?

Have we had to survive being
'civilized' by your disaster
on nature, you,
Mr. Cult
Mr. Klan
Mr. Clandestine
Mr. Nighttime
Doublelife
Sheriff during the day Grand Dragon at night?

Do your daughters slide forward full of truth
swallowed whole like eggs;
then renege and press fleshly white thumbs
down on our wind pipes hissing: don't tell don't tell?
They say 'don't tell' like you're going to will them
something besides the death of the planet.

postscript 1958

The black child feels the wind blowing backwards,
turns the tv off; tries to tell her mother something.

California Dreamin'

Was I this lonely as a child
My bones are lonely now.
Pointing to a white flag with a brown bear on it
the teacher tells us this is our state flag.
In my class everybody is born in America.
We pledge allegiance to the flag
of the United States.
The teacher tells us the Sequoia is our state tree
that they are the tallest trees in the world.
I wonder about a boy I knew in kindergarten
so short he had trouble climbing into
his seat. Is he lonely now like
a ferris wheel abandoned in the rain.
As a child I liked those things—ferris wheels,
cotton candy, crinolines, the Mouseketeers.
I wonder was my brother always lonely? Ever?
Was he lonely in the park when the killer came?
When god erased his name could he feel it,
was he lonely?
Was he cold the night, the years, he walked alone?
Did he think about his childhood? Did he think
he was insane?
Did the voices writing in the wind
comfort him or drive him like a shepherd
over concrete collecting aluminum cans?
Did he breathe his own blood like a blanket finally
covering him?

Can we lay down together now like I always wanted
    since
I am so lonely and he is bones?
The Golden Poppy is our state flower.
California is the second largest state in the Union.
The teacher? Where is she now?
Is she old? Dead? Did she die from drinking
or complete twenty-five years of talking to lonely
    desperate
old people in baby bodies about the kinds
of clouds, arithmetic, verbs, George Washington.
Did she know we would end up rainy eyes,
homeless, wandering through state forests
trying to find the trees she taught us were ours?

1989/Gorilla in the Midst #1

"Move," he wills, his face turning red under the weight
    of his penis
laying limp beyond will or desire. His wife sighs.
He can't stand her, fat bitch. "I find your weight gain
    a total
turnoff," he cut. "You look like a fat pig," hard. Her
    face

disintegrates like a graphic on a computer screen
into little pieces that get smaller, further apart and
    escape
carrying him back to the dream he is running from—
    his son calling him,
the leaves fluttering outside the bedroom window like
    long green tongues,

"Hey Dad," the high-pitched voice clear like a bell, a
    girl or a faggot
pulls him, "Come look," and the boy cast off the blue
    coverlet to reveal
his penis, erect and bubble-gum pink, pulsating in his
    young hands.
"Pretty soon you'll be able to bust a few cherries!" he
    guffaws then

slaps the boy's back so hard it breaks into pieces that
    slide

down the air like her lips on his penis, "Atta girl," he
   was getting hard
dee har har hard! He grabbed her, jam! Damn! No
   action.
He tried again but it was like trying to nail jello to a
   fence now.

Splat, against the hairy hard of her blonde hell. She
   stunk.
She was a pig! He pinched her thigh hard,
"You used to be something to look at."
Cracks in her face deepen to seismic crevices that

break into pieces that get familiarly smaller and smaller,
finally disintegrating to nothing left except the solitary
   black
hole of one eye that is the half life of the other eye
sitting devoid of everything except decomposition.

      BAM!
"You don't have to hit me!" she screamed.
"Shutup bitch!"
"No I won't! You don't have to take it out on me cause
   you can't get it up!"
"Shaddup!   You stupid bitch!   Shut up!"
     BAM!   BAM!   BAM!   BAM!

1965/Gorilla in the Midst #2

"How'd niggers get black?" he asked.
"God poured black paint on 'em for fucking
    monkeys!" Buddy hooted
as Johnny turned the corner
into the school parking lot. Wonder
who he was gonna take
to the prom.
The Blonde, or
red
head peggy
sue, or donna

donna the prima donna
he would be her johnny angel
oh, how she would love him.
How he was gonna feel
walking into the gymnasium with those tits. Shit!
That bitch had tits, big tits.
He was gonna be late for his first class,
again, O.K. math, he had done O.K. in math;
English, he had barely passed.
College?
No.
C-minus don't go
to college.
A job, maybe
the army. The draft?
He didn't want to get drafted

did he?

Or did he?

He wasn't no flat-foot homo hippy resister Jew.

Yes! He would go! Fuck it, now that he had thought
   about it,

his mind was made up, he was gonna enlist.

Better 'n being a pinko queer

or twenty years

twenty years on the day shifting

to night at the aircraft plant making,

like his dad, making

toilet seats for airplanes.

"I enlisted." His father reached for the bowl of green
   peas passing in

silence around the table. "Idiot!" his mother screamed.
   "Have you

lost your mind? Have you? HAVE YOU!" His sister
   rose to the command,

"Bring me a beer," before the words were out his father's
   mouth.

He remembered that as a kid peas had made him want
   to throw up;

now their green void filled his mouth and slid down his
   throat with ease.

Buddy slams his locker, looks at him

like he's crazy, "What'd you do some shit like that for!"

Buddy's eyes like a foreign country

covered with ice. The eyes too blue, colored

like the turquoise jewelry of the one-eighth Indian

Buddy had once bragged he was.
"What are you staring at man?" Buddy snarled.
"Nothing," he mumbled their bodies
breaking the surface of forgotten water
like long blond pink fish,
him and Buddy since
first grade.

Like that he's back teetering
on the edge of six years old his eyes
seeing the bottom of the pool;
and if he hadn't been a child
his heart woulda stopped when he fell
off the edge of the deep end
into emptiness, into cement hard
and painted turquoise, cracked
at the bottom, his bone
pushing through
the blood colored sky,
raining.

128

His mind
was like an elevator
going down.
Shit! They had made such a stink
how could he tell 'em he wasn't sure. If
they would just leave him the fuck
alone,
he would know what to do.
"You're a fool!"
"'Cause I love my country!"
"Fool!"
Honestly, he hadn't thought about
the fucker one way or the other.
His country? Sure it was great
America was great would always be great.
Down, yeah man
all the way.
"When she comes out the laundry room,"
Steven said.
"But she'll have all those clothes," Johnny protested.
Steven's father was Jewish, a dentist.
"So that's when we get her, on the way to the living
   room
with the clothes." Steven should know,
it was his house.
"Let her get to the living room first," Buddy said.
Buddy's father was a part-Cherokee memory.

"Yeah."
"Yeah."
"Yeah."
One after the other they all agreed.
BAP!
Buddy slapped her once.
Hard.
Down on his belly Steven crawled
over the living room carpet like a soldier
under fire to the windows
shutting the blinds and drapes.
Just the idea of Johnny being around a dentist's
son, even if he was Jewish,
made his mother happy.

His turn to climb on top
her stained brown thighs.
He kneads his dick
like soft dough.
He looks at her small
and scared to paralysis
and feels his dick
get hard. Pushes in—
she's wet with them.
He can smell their sperm
tiny fish swimming on her thighs
Carmen
Rosita
Maria,
what the fuck,
bitch!

He bends
down
bites through her lip
till his teeth meet.
Her eyes bulge out
his mouth fills with
blood he spits
in her face. Steven's jaw drops open.
He thrusts his dick
in again, pretends
she's Steven; the thought
sends shivers
up his back.
He closes his eyes,
trips to another world,
warm all over,
he feels wonderful, his chest
opens and he lets out a yodel
unashamed hillbilly
yee oowww!
Fuck Steven
Fuck Buddy too
injun half-breed, Jew.
He was WHITE.
His dick was in.
For the first time
in his life
he really felt
something.

why'd they send him to
Dr. Zimmerman? All he'd said was
he couldn't sleep. He didn't need a psychiatrist—
he just couldn't sleep is all.
"Is that all?" Dr. Zimmerman probed.
Johnny sees the black boy,
all his lights popped from C-7 down,
singing,
his voice rising
out a foxhole like steam
from a morning shit in the woods.

132 He looks into the doctor's eyes coiling
opposite him, like
snakes, waiting;
and laughs.
"What's funny, Johnny?" Dr. Zimmerman pleads. He
needs words for the book he is writing.
"Nothing," Johnny says.
"Nothing, Johnny?" He switches from psychiatric
supplicant to dealer, "I can get you something to get
to sleep."
"I . . ."
"Yes John," perspiration popped out on Dr Zimmer-
   man's
top lip, "I'm listening."
"I . . ."
"Go on," he hisses.

"I wanna . . . wanna pee . . . be," Johnny stutters,
"a policeman."
Bewildered the doctor scowls, "Huh?"
"Join the force get married have kids," Johnny spurts
clasping his hands together
like white chains. He looked at
Dr. Zimmerman's nose poised like a beagle
in hunting air, and
he wanted to say, 'Doctor.'
He wanted to say, 'Doctor, my dick won't get hard.'
He wanted to say, 'Doctor, my dick won't get hard.'
But he couldn't. He couldn't.
He just could not say that. So,
he reached for the white paper
the prescription was written on
and watched himself walk out
on water, a hard pink river,
that was really his tongue,
stretching out in front of him
forever.

133

A tube was
coming out
his nose
and one was
stuck in his dick.
Johnson, black boys
called it.
Peter
prick
cock
schlong
bone
pecker
rod
ding-a-ling
dong
thing
umm, what else? 'Wee wee,' she had called it, "Put your
wee wee away honey. We don't play with
our wee wee at the
dinner table." *We*? Did she have one? Where did you
play with it? You don't, she said,
ever.
It was bad
a blind snake.
"Doctor."
"Yes Johnny," Dr. Zimmerman breathed in the good

feeling of control.

I.V. bags wobbled like square blobs of jello on top of aluminum poles. The sunlight on the linoleum floor was cut into stripes by bars on the window.

The radio crooned long, blonde.

"Doctor."

"I'm listening Johnny."

"I'm not a man."

"Not a man?"

"I mean my johnson won't get hard," Johnny said.

Flies buzzed around the black boy's body. The singing had stopped a long time ago.

The smell was terrible.

Dr. Zimmerman was joyous with choice and knowing.

"Psychotherapy," he stated.

"Huh!"

"What do you mean by 'huh,' Johnny?" Dr. Zimmerman asked.

"I mean what's psychotherapy?"

"It's the treatment of a mental disorder by psychological means, for example, discussion, explanation—"

"*Mental* disorder?"

"Well," Dr. Zimmerman looked at the words written on the paper clipped to his official looking clipboard, "Your exact words were, 'Doctor my johnson won't get hard,' this I think, is mental Johnny, what do you think?"

A dream he hasn't had yet happens and ends in darkness.

"I've helped thousands of men over the years over-
come
all kinds of problems and I can help you."
Oh no, he thought.
The crooning from the radio rises like flood waters.
"I mean just telling me what you told me earlier
has helped you, hasn't it?"
"No."
"You know we can commit you John."
"Jezus Christ! What the fuck are you talking about?
Commit me for what!"
"For your own good Johnny. You're a very disturbed
young man—"
"What the fuck!" Johnny yelped.
"You tried to take your own life. That is very serious."
The doctor patted him very gently, his soft white
hand heavy on Johnny's thigh.
"Johnny, I think we have a lot to talk about, don't
you?"

"You shouldn't'a married me."

He felt like beating her to death. Stupid, sausage head, bitch.

"You knew you had this problem when we got married."

"Porky the Pig is upset," he sneered.

Her face reddened. "Making fun of me may make you feel better—"

"I'm sorry."

"I'm not," she paused. "Porky Pig, Fat Slob, Big Ben, whatever,

it doesn't make any difference what you call me anymore,
I know what I am, I'm a woman and I thought I was
marrying a man."

137

"You saying—" anger choked the words in his throat, where did this bitch

get off talking to *him* like that, "You saying I ain't
no man!"

"I want you to get some kind of counseling," firmly,
"or I want a divorce."

"Divorce? Get a divorce! See who wants your fat ass!"

BAP!   SLAP!   SLAP!

She screamed, the hole of her mouth filled with blood.
"God help me!" she gasped at her teeth like white fish
floating out of her mouth onto the floor. God I gotta

get—

BAM! BAM! BAM! BAM!
BAM! BAM! BAM! BAM!
BAM! BAM! BAM! BAM!

He loked at her bloody and still like a run-over animal;
the slight movement of her chest rising to inhale
refueled his anger—

look at what she had made him do god dammit! God
damn!

Big bullets of sweat popped out on his brow. It was
hot.

He had to get out of the room, house. He was 40 years
old. Married

16 years, 2 kids. 5 times in 16 years, at least the kids
but 1 dies.

5 times, then the desert years. Nothing, years and
years, nothing.

Wild Thing

And I'm running,
running wild
running free,
like soldiers down
the beach,
like someone
just threw me
the ball.
My thighs pump
thru the air
like tires
rolling down
the highway
big & round
eating up the ground
of America
but I never been any
further than 42nd Street.
Below that is as
unfamiliar as my
father's face,
foreign as the smell of
white girls' pussy,
white girls on TV
My whole world is
black & brown & closed,
till I open it

with a rock,
christen it with
blood.
BOP BOP
the music
pops thru me
like electric shocks,
my sweat is a
river running
thru my liver
green with hate,
my veins bulge out
like tomorrow,
my dick is
the Empire State Building,
I eat your fear
like a chimpanzee
ow ow
ow whee
ow!
My sneakers glide off
the cement like
white dreams
looking out at the world
thru a cage of cabbage
& my mother's fat,
hollering don't do this
& don't do that.
I scream against the restraint
of her big ass sitting on my face
drowning my dreams in sameness.

I'm scared to go
it hurts me to stay.
She sits cross-legged
in front the TV
telling me no
feeding me
clothing me
bathing me in her ugliness
high high in the sky
18th floor of the projects.
Her welfare check buys me $85 sneakers
but can't buy me a father.
She makes cornbread from Jiffy box mix
buys me a coat
$400, leather like everybody else's.
I wear the best, man!
14 karat gold chain
I take off before I go wildin'.
Fuck you nigger!
Nobody touches my gold!
My name is Leroy
L-E-R-O-Y
bold gold
I got the goods
that make the ladies
young & old
sign your name across my heart
I want you to be my baby
Rapper D
Rapper G
Rapper *I*

my name is lightning
across the sky
So what I can't read
you spozed to teach me
you the teacher
I'm the ape
black ape
in white sneakers
hah hah
I rape
rape
rape
I do the wild thing
I do the wild thing.

My teacher asks me
what would I do
if I had 6 months
to live.
I tell her I'd fuck her,
sell dope & do the wild thing.
My thighs are locomotives
hurling me thru the
underbrush of Central Park,
the jungle.
I either wanna be a cop
or the biggest dope dealer in Harlem
when I grow up.
I feel good!
It's a man's world,
my sound is king
I am the black man's sound.

Get off my face whining bitch!
No, I didn't go to school today
& I ain't goin' tomorrow!
I like how the sky looks
when I'm running,
my clothes are new & shiny,
my tooth gleams gold.
I'm fast as a wolf
I need a rabbit,
the sky is falling
calling my name
Leroy Leroy.
I look up
blood bust
in my throat

it's my homeboys
L.D., C.K. & Beanbutt!
Hey man what's up!
I got the moon
in my throat,
I remember when
Christ sucked my dick
behind the pulpit,
I was 6 years old
he made me promise
not to tell no one.
I eat cornbread &
collard greens.
I only wear Adidas
I'm my own man,
they can wear New Balance or Nike

if they want,
I wear Adidas.
I'm L.D.
lover
mover
man with the money
all the girls know me.
I'm classified as mildly retarded
but I'm not
least I don't think
I am.
Special Education classes
eat up my brain
like last week's greens
rotting in plastic containers.

My mother never
throws away anything.
I could kill her
I could kill her
all those years
all those years
I sat
I sat in classes
for the mentally retarded
so she could get
the extra money welfare gives
for retarded kids.
So she could get
some money,
some motherfuckin' money.
That bitch

that bitch
I could kill her
all the years
I sat next to kids
who shitted on themselves,
dreaming amid
rooms of dull eyes
that one day
my rhymes
would break open
the sky
& my name would
be written
across the marquee
at the Apollo

in bold gold
me bigger
than Run DMC
Rapper G
Rapper O
Rapper *Me*
"Let's go!" I scream.
My dick is a locomotive
my sister eats like a 50¢ hot dog.
I scream, "I *said* let's go!"
"It's 40 of us
a black wall of sin.
The god of our fathers
descends down & blesses us,
I say thank you Jesus.
Now let's do the

wild thing.
I pop off the cement
like toast outta toaster
hot hard crumbling
running
running
the park is green
combat operation
lost soul
looking for Lt. Calley
Jim Jones
anybody who could direct
this spurt of semen
rising to the sky.

soldiers
flying thru
the rhythm
"Aw man!
nigger please
nigger
nigger
nigger.
I know
who I am."
My soul sinks
to its knees &
howls under the
moon rising full,
"Let's get a female jogger!"
I shout into the twilight
looking at the

middle-class thighs
pumping past me,
cadres of bitches
who deserve to die
for thinking they're better
than me.
You ain't better than
nobody bitch.
The rock begs my hand
to hold it.
It says, "Come on man."
T.W., Pit Bull, J.D. & me
grab the bitch
ugly big nose white bitch
but she's beautiful cause she's white
she's beautiful cause she's skinny
she's beautiful cause she's gonna die
cause her daddy's gonna cry
Bitch!
I bring the rock down
on her head
sounds dull & flat
like the time I busted
the kitten's head.
The blood is real & red
my dick rises.
I tear off her bra
feel her perfect pink breasts
like Brooke Shields
like bitches in Playboy
Shit! I come all over myself!

I bring the rock down
the sound has rhythm
hip hop ain't gonna stop
till your face sees
what I see every day
walls of blood
walls of blood
she's wriggling like
a pig in the mud.
I never seen a pig
or a cow
'cept on TV.
Her nipples are like
hard strawberries
my mouth tastes
like pesticide.
I fart.
Yosef slams her
across the face with a pipe.
My dick won't get
hard no more.
I bring the rock down
removing what she
looks like forever
ugly bitch
ugly bitch
I get up
blood on my hands
semen in my jeans
the sky is black
the trees are green

I feel good baby
I just did
the *wild thing*!

Strange Juice (or the murder
of Latasha Harlins)

I REMEMBER MY boyfriend, the dark behind the brown of his eyes and how he look in his leather. I was walking with that good feeling thinking about him, the next day of school—maybe I go, maybe I don't. You know, who gives a fuck. And nothing special, you know, nothing is so special except now I'm dead. It's the day I died. And the sky was red-brown gauze. You could see patches of blue if you look up but I don't hardly ever look up. My eyes on the ground checking out my feet in orange Reeboks. What else I remember? Now that I look back it seems like the collard greens piled up on plywood boards at the door was huge green tears that tried to warn me. The day was the same but different. I didn't do nothin'. I slid open the glass door of the refrigerator that keeps all the beverages cool, it's so hot here. My eyes glance up at the camera pointed like a gun from the corner of the wall. Fuck it. I slip the cold bottle of orange juice in my backpack, go to the counter. I'll get some gum, if she say something I'll say, aw bitch I was gonna buy this juice, you think I'm stupid. Wonder what we gonna do in school tomorrow. I be so glad to get out the ninth grade, go to high school. If I'm late for homeroom one more time—

"Oh bitch please! I was gonna pay for—OOG FU WOO SHIT SUE! Speak English hoe! Take your damn juice. I wasn't stealing nothin' from you chink ass hoe!"

She grabbed me. Bitch! I hit that hoe upside her jaw. Who the fuck she think she is putting her hands on somebody. Fuck this hoe, I ain't gon' argue with this bitch. I turn my back. And I walk away. I see the collard greens again only now they're growing like big trees then I see a red dirt road in the middle of the salad bar, no lie, like I'm high or something. Then everything is normal Koreatown fruit stand again. Del Monte corn out of a can poured in a stainless steel tub, iceberg, romaine, bran muffins and brownies wrapped in clear plastic. Fuck it I'm not thirsty no way.

1.

I don't hear the blast till I'm dead
I don't feel nothin' either
as I split in half
a dog yelps
and every sound I ever heard
flies out my mouth on green wings.
Crimson waterfalls open in my skull
and my bones come aloose,
the dog is screaming
like a siren now
and in the distance a bucket of water
spills over on a dusty red dirt road
and my heart quits
falls face first in
shattered glass on a
concrete floor.
The camera keeps
rolling.
My left leg twitches.
I don't cry.
Fifteen.
Green as greens
passing from sight
under broken bottles of light.

2.

I don't remember what I did wrong.
Somebody hit you, you hit 'em back.
She didn't have to shoot me.
I was born here
and someone can shoot me and go home
and eat turkey on Thanksgiving—
what kinda shit is that?
Videotape the bitch killing me,
the hoe's own videotape
recording
the end of my days
reeling obscenely
for tv cameras—
my blood
sweet Jesus!
Rolling 20s
Bounty Hunters
PJs
Imperial Courts
NWA
LAPD
South Central
Hollywood
18th Street Diamond Riders
Easy Riders
it's a brown thing

it's a black thing
Crips
Bloods, Mexicans together forever tonight.
I don't remember . . .
I jus' wanted some juice
and now I'm dead.
Killed by a model minority
success story.
Listen, is anybody gonna
say anything?
I was gonna get a new orange leather jacket
to match my Reeboks.
I was passing math *and*
doing good in English.

Fuck history, I'm tired of hearing
'bout George Washington
and Columbus.
I told that cracker, "Shit, mutherfucker
what about us?"
No, I *wasn't* pregnant,
but I was gonna have a baby,
definitely, one day.
I like Luther Vandross, Tone-Lōc
and Queen Latifah.
Listen, is anybody gonna
say anything?
Community service!
A white bitch
with a pink slit
between her legs

Breaking Karma #3

1.

From where I sit I can see the yellow gray
stains in the crotch of my mother's underpants.
She leans back against the headboard of the bed
withered thighs cocked open drinking whiskey straight.

The smell from between her legs permeates the summer
   air.
I am turning thru her photograph album when the
   medal
fallen to the inner spine of the book hits my eye.
   Stunned I ask,
"What's this?" She cackles like the witch in Hansel and
   Gretel,

like "stop acting bitch," and says, "You know what it
   is." I turn away,
stare at skeins of synthetic wool tangled orange and
   green around
knitting needles and empty bottles spilling from paste-
   board boxes
near her bed. Finally, I ask. "Where did you get it?"

The room's one tiny window is painted shut. Gloating,
   she looks
at me with such triumph and glee, "I was guarding a
   prisoner

during the war. A German fella and he liked me. So I
    told him, you know,
give me something, something that means something
    to you."

2.

If I was an artist I would paint a room piss-yellow
with huge knitting needles suspended from the ceiling
    dripping
blood or milk like long steel teats. On the far wall of
    the yellow room
would be a photograph of me, my mother and her
    Nazi medal.

Breaking Karma #4

1.

My eyes travel down the row of neatly filed journals
until I get to the one I kept at that time: 4/15/83–
    10/18/83.
I pore over the pages but can't find anything like that,
    like:
my mother got drunk and told me she wished I had
    never been born.

2.

I am an artist painting a woman flat on her back.
bent knees up, dark thighs spread apart on a bed, in a
    cobalt
blue room of roaches, mice and peeling paint. Her torso
    and
face are shrouded with a sheet spattered with dried
    blood. A chair,
lamp and poster on the wall, *Ethel Waters: AFRICANA:
    Something*
New In A Colored Review, place the scene in the 1940s.
The colors are dark and subdued except for the woman's
    scarlet
tipped fingers holding her brilliant pink vagina open
for the coat hanger's steel hook.

One Day

All week my period plays at coming
then leaves me bewildered staring
in my panties at faint brown stains
I haven't seen in 30 years.
Is this the end? As it was in the
beginning (brown stains in cotton underwear)
so shall it be in the end?

It never crossed my mind it would hurt—
no long-legged daughters to hate me
or call me old-fashioned or outta style
or to say like white girls on TV, "Gee Mom
you just don't understand," that it
would stretch my heart out
of shape like this, mark my smile
draw such rings under my eyes.
No one ever told me, I never knew
to be part of the counterculture
would be so lonely.

I felt for so long I had to save my own life,
no use in two of us drowning.
And then there was the ABUSE, how it left me
uncomfortable with a naked infant on my lap,
how I was afraid of descending down
to lick the little clitoris or of sticking
my finger up its vagina between diaper changes.
I mean this is what was done to me.

All my life the sound of a child crying
like fingernails raking down a blackboard
twisted something inside of me till it snapped
screaming: shut up shut up SHUT THE FUCK UP!
And I would want to slap, punch, stomp
throw it out the window or in a pot of boiling water—
anything! to get it to stop that
stop that goddamn motherfucking crying!

Then I work.
I work years
in a circle
in a group
in a journal
alone.
I heave, crawl, vomit, abreact, 12 step, psycho-this,
    therapy-that,
anger workshops, homeopathy, crystals—
all on poverty wages.

And I remember
a man so mean
so different from the face in photographs
and home movies.
I remember a woman with
red fingernails like razors
up my vagina.
I cry
shake
face the impossible,

write it
tell it.

I can't see any change.
Just all my time, money and
most of my youth spent,
and shelves of books: "The Best kept Secret,"
"Prisoners of Childhood," "Kiss Daddy Goodnight,"
"The Courage to Heal," "Father-Daughter Incest."
Then one day the woman downstairs,
her with the dope smell escaping
from under the door's dark face,
takes in a baby for money.
And often under the deafening boom boom
of music so loud it sounds like a cannon
168 being fired I hear a baby crying.

One day it's just a crying and a crying
but instead of wanting to bash its head
on the sidewalk I relax, I relax all over
and a warm pink glow expands around my heart
like in some new age instruction book for meditation,
and I whisper, if that baby was mine
I would just hold it, hold it and hold it, 11 hours
if it took that long, till it stopped crying.
If that baby was mine I say slowly
and see the tiny child body safe in my warm brown
    arms.
If it was mine, I whisper again.
Maybe the baby hears me cause the crying
downstairs, in my soul, stops as I hold
my work, the work of a lifetime close to me.

Notes

in my father's house

ON MAY 13, 1985, Wilson Goode, Philadelphia's first black mayor, ordered a firebomb dropped on 6221 Osage Avenue, a house occupied by Move, a back-to-nature group of African Americans who rejected modern technology and adopted the surname Africa. The bombing and resultant fire killed eleven people, including children, and destroyed sixty-one homes in the neighborhood. (*New York Times*, May 14–16, 1985)

From *Bad Blood: The Tuskegee Syphilis Experiment*, by James H. Jones (The Free Press, 1981): "In 1972 it was discovered that for forty years the United States Public Health service had been conducting a study of the effects of untreated syphilis on black men in Macon County, Alabama, in and around the county seat of Tuskegee. This study was conducted despite the fact that the germ that causes syphilis, the stages of the disease's development, and the complications that can result from untreated syphilis were all known to medical science in 1932—the year the Tuskegee Study began.

"Involved with the study from the beginning was a black nurse, Eunice Rivers, who served as the liaison between the researchers and the subjects. She served as a facilitator, bridging the many barriers that stemmed from the educational and cultural gap between the physicians and the subjects. Most important, the men trusted her."

poem for jennifer, marla, tawana & me

Lisa Steinberg was murdered by Joel Steinberg, a white middle-class lawyer, who had illegally adopted her. On January 30, 1989, after one of most publicized trials in New York City, Joel Steinberg was convicted of first-degree manslaughter for allowing his illegally adopted daughter's life to seep away after beating her—a beating that occurred up to eleven hours before help was called.

"What first signaled to me that a Black girl was about to become a public victim was hearing the *name* of an alleged rape victim—Tawana Brawley—given on a local radio news show. Since when does the press give the name of any rape victim much less one who is underage? Obviously when the victim is Black . . ." (Audrey Edwards, *Essence*, November 1988)

"Tawana Brawley is a liar and her advisers should be punished for perpetuating the Big Lie, enraged state Attorney General Robert Abrams charged yesterday . . .

"The controversial case came to a close in the packed National Guard Armory in Poughkeepsie where a grand jury had met and decided that the teenager was never abducted or raped . . .

"The case began Nov. 24, 1987, when the Brawley family reported she had disappeared from her former home in Wappinger Falls in Dutchess County, New York.

"She was found four days later in a plastic bag, with racial epithets scrawled on her chest and dog feces smeared over her body." (Bill Hoffman and Esther Pessin, *New York Post*, October 7, 1988)

"When the special prosecutor (David Sall) resigned (saying he had a conflict of interest), Dutchess County Judge Judith Hillary expressed telling concern. She was quoted saying the Brawley case was going to be very difficult because all of the subjects were from "our most prominent law enforcement families." (*Daily News*, June 10, 1988)

Utrice C. Leid reports in the *City Sun*, July 6–12, 1988, in a feature article entitled *The Brawley Case: A Series of 'Coincidences'*:

". . . According to documents from Saint Francis Hospital that the *City Sun* has obtained, George M. Brazzale, an arson investigator for the Dutchess County Sheriff's office, had signed the hospital records as the investigator in charge of Tawana's case at the time.

"Brazzale apparently was present at 3 p.m., roughly about half an hour after Tawana was admitted . . . Brazzale apparently was present also at 4 p.m. when the nursing log read: 'Police present. Pictures taken.'

"A 4:30 p.m., even though Tawana had been diagnosed by that time as being a victim of 'possibly sexual assault,' she was given a 'complete bath'—three and a half hours before a rape test and internal examination were done . . .

"By 8 p.m. Brazzale was in possession of all the tangible and obtainable physical evidence connected with the case. He had the specimens taken for the rape test . . .

"To whom did Brazzale take this evidence? What became of it?

"COINCIDENCE NO. 1: Brazzale, who is now on vacation, is the chief arson investigator in the Dutchess County Sherriff's office. Steve A. Pagones, named by Brawley's lawyers as a key suspect in the case, is an assistant Dutchess County district attorney who is in charge of arson prosecutions.

" 'Steve works closely with George,' Dutchess County District Attorney William Grady told the *Poughkeepsie Journal* . . .

"COINCIDENCE NO. 2: Brazzale got the rape kit and other evidence on Nov. 28; they supposedly were turned directly over to the Federal bureau of Investigation for analysis.

". . . The *Poughkeepsie Journal* last week quoted sources within the sheriff's office as saying that the rape test 'may have been kept for a brief period at department headquarters' but that it was received 'undisturbed' by the F.B.I.

". . . the third coincidence involves one of the men the Brawley lawyers and advisors have identified as being involved in the brutal kidnapping-rape of Tawana Brawley. Harry J. Crist, 28, was a part-time police officer who moonlighted as an IBM assembly plant worker.

"COINCIDENCE NO. 3: The *New York Times* in an article titled 'Figures in Brawley Case: Allegations Without Proof' reported April 9 that Crist 'worked at his two jobs, on patrol and at IBM' the day Tawana had disappeared . . .

"In fact, a review of Crist's tour-of-duty police file shows that he *did not* report for his 5 p.m.-to-midnight shift on Nov. 24. Further, Crist's file, verified by Chief Donald F. Williams of the town of Fishkill police department, shows Crist reported for work for only one day after the 24th—on the 25th—and never again after that. He was said to have committed suicide with his service revolver 4 days after Tawana was found . . .

"COINCIDENCE NO. 4: The person who discovered Crist dead in his apartment was Scott Patterson, a close friend with whom he allegedly had spent sometime on Nov. 27 and 28. Patterson, a 26-year-old state trooper, retrieved Crist's alleged suicide note and his gun—this means he disturbed the scene by removing key pieces of evidence—and took it directly to Steve Pagones . . .

"COINCIDENCE NO. 5: Pagones, Patterson and Crist

have since told authorities that between the time
Tawana disappeared and the time she was found they
had been together socially . . ."

Strange Juice

From *How We Got to This Point: An Asian Pacific
Perspective on the Los Angeles Rebellion*, by Scott Kura-
shige (*forward motion*, July 1992, vol. 11, no. 3, p. 10):
"In an extremely high-profile incident, a fifteen-year-
old African-American girl, Latasha Harlins, was shot in
the back of the head and killed by Korean merchant
Soon Ja Du. Black real-estate developer Danny Bakewell
organized a boycott of the store, but was frequently
accused of grandstanding. Though the incident occurred
before the Rodney King beating, the videotape showing
the killing was released by police after the King video
had been shown repeatedly. In what was arguably an
effort to direct attention and criticism away from the
police and the King incident, the videotape of Du
shooting Harlins was shown on television continually for
several months.

"Du was convicted of voluntary manslaughter, and a
white Republican-appointed judge, Joyce Karlan, sen-
tenced her to probation and community service. Karlan
rejected the probation department's suggested sixteen-
year prison sentence and manipulated the case to make
her own ideological statement. Drawing upon both the
'model minority myth' and Nathan Glazer's 'immigrant

theory' stating that anybody can make it in America, Karlan painted a picture of Du as a hard-working merchant who was justifiably scared of African-American criminals. Karlan's outlandish adjudicating inflamed racial tensions between African and Korean Americans."

SERPENT'S TAIL

HIGH RISK BOOKS